From Your Friends at The MAILBOX®

I CAN MAKE IT! I CAN READ IT!

20 Reproducible Booklets to Develop Early Literacy Skills

Grade 1

SUMMER

WRITTEN BY:
Nancy Anderson, Linda Morgason, Jan Robbins

EDITED BY:
Mary Lester
Kim T. Griswell

ILLUSTRATED BY:
Mary Lester

COVER DESIGN BY:
Nick Greenwood and Kimberly Richard

www.themailbox.com

CHILDREN'S AND PARENTS' SERVICES
PATCHOGUE-MEDFORD LIBRARY

©2000 by THE EDUCATION CENTER, INC.
All rights reserved.

ISBN# 1-56234-435-8

Except as provided for herein, no part of this publication may be reproduced or transmitted in any form or by any means, electronic or mechanical, including photocopying, recording, or storing in any information storage and retrieval system or electronic online bulletin board, without prior written permission from The Education Center, Inc. Permission is given to the original purchaser to reproduce patterns and reproducibles for individual classroom use only and not for resale or distribution. Reproduction for an entire school or school system is prohibited. Please direct written inquiries to The Education Center, Inc., P.O. Box 9753, Greensboro, NC 27429-0753. The Education Center®, *The Mailbox*®, and the mailbox/post/grass logo are registered trademarks of The Education Center, Inc. All other brand or product names are trademarks or registered trademarks of their respective companies.

Manufactured in the United States
10 9 8 7 6 5 4 3 2 1

TABLE OF CONTENTS

Special to Me (Father's Day) 3

Splish! Splash! (Pool Safety) 7

Mmm! Mmm! Ice Cream! 11

A Taste of Watermelon 15

Family Fun 19

What Might You See? (Fourth of July) 25

Oh, Goody! It's a Picnic! 31

A-camping We Will Go! 35

Let's Go on Vacation! 39

Butterfly or Moth? 45

Cobras-s-s! 51

Down on the Farm 55

Going on Safari! 59

Deep, Deep, Deeper (Ocean Animals) 63

Howdy, Partner! (Old West) 67

City Views Apartments 73

A Walk in the Country 77

Storm Watch! 83

Up in the Air Over Planes 87

Rock On! 93

SPECIAL TO ME

Dress up your reading and writing program with this heartwarming Father's Day booklet! Give each student a copy of pages 4–6. Have her color and cut out her booklet backing, cover, and pages. (Remind students to color lightly over the text so that the booklet can be read.) Then read the booklet pages with students. Instruct the student to write a response about her dad (or other male caregiver) to complete the appropriate sentences. Next, have her stack her booklet pages in numerical order, placing the cover on top. Staple the pages to the backing where indicated. Invite each youngster to read her booklet to the class. Then encourage her to take her booklet home to read and give to her special someone. You can be sure dads will love these ties!

CREATIVE DECORATING OPTIONS

- Glue rickrack or sequins to the cover tie.
- Outline the cover tie with glitter glue.

Special to Me

To extend this booklet-making activity, read to students Laura Joffe Numeroff's *What Daddies Do Best* (Simon & Schuster Books for Young Readers, 1998).

Booklet Backing and Cover

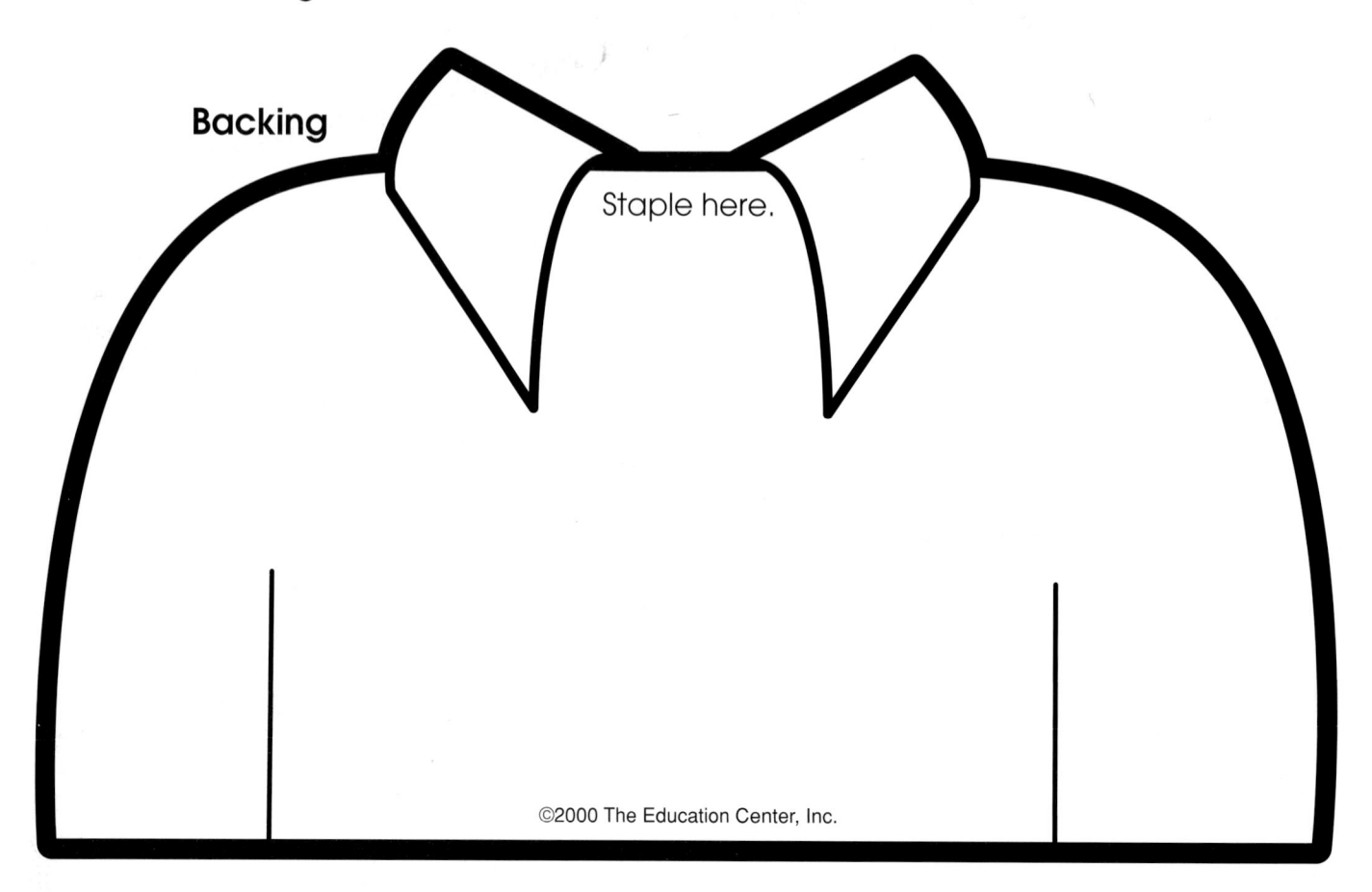

Backing

Staple here.

©2000 The Education Center, Inc.

Cover

Special to Me

©2000 The Education Center, Inc. • *I Can Make It! I Can Read It!* • *Summer* • TEC3508

Note to the teacher: Use with "Special to Me" on page 3.

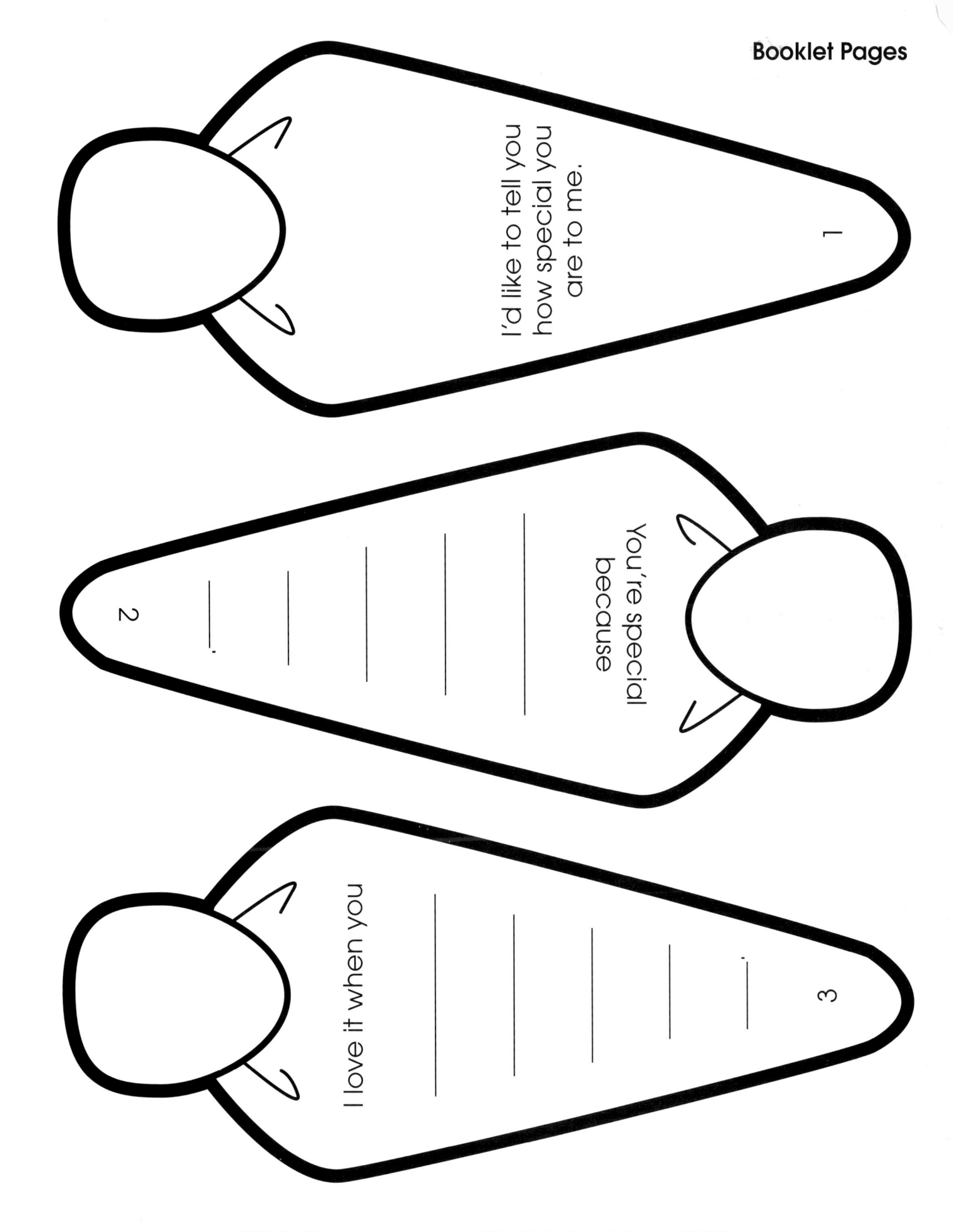

Booklet Pages

I'd like to tell you how special you are to me.

1

You're special because _____

2

I love it when you _____

3

©2000 The Education Center, Inc. • *I Can Make It! I Can Read It!* • *Summer* • TEC3508

Note to the teacher: Use with "Special to Me" on page 3.

5

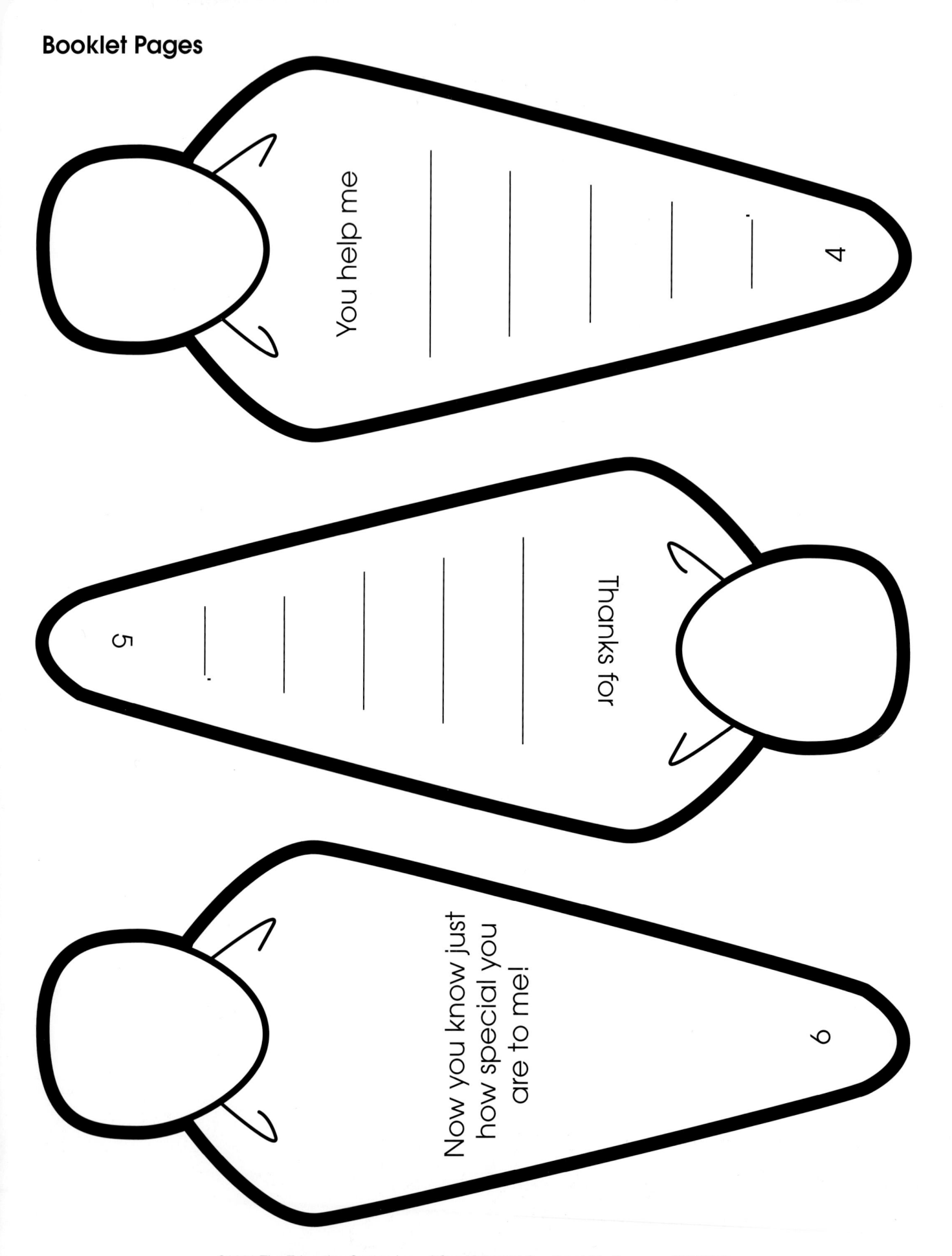

Booklet Pages

You help me _____.

4

Thanks for _____.

5

Now you know just how special you are to me!

6

SPLISH! SPLASH!

Dive into reading with this step booklet on pool safety! Give each student a copy of pages 8–10. Have the student color and cut out her booklet backing, pages, and patterns. (Remind students to color lightly over the text so the booklet can be read.) Then help the student cut the slits on the backing. Next, instruct her to fold the otter boxes along the thin lines. Direct her to insert the bottom half of each otter through its appropriate slit (see the illustration below) and then unfold the boxes. Have her staple each booklet page to the left-hand side of the backing as illustrated. Then read a completed booklet with students, demonstrating how to make the boy otter swim back and forth and the girl otter bob up and down. Provide time for each student to read her booklet with a partner before she takes it home to read with family members.

CREATIVE DECORATING OPTIONS

- To create the effect of pool water, use watercolors to paint the booklet pages and backing.
- On the back of a booklet page, glue a construction paper beach ball halfway below the waterline so that it appears to be in the pool.

To extend this booklet activity, invite a lifeguard to visit the class to talk about pool safety.

Booklet Backing

Splish! Splash!

Place the girl otter here.

Place the boy otter here.

6. Look out for other swimmers.
7. Keep your hands to yourself while in the pool.
8. Do not splash other swimmers in the face.
9. If swimming in a pool with a lifeguard, do what he or she tells you to do.
10. Do not chew gum while swimming.

Splish! Splash! Keep cool this summer by swimming safely.

©2000 The Education Center, Inc. • *I Can Make It! I Can Read It!* • Summer • TEC3508

Note to the teacher: Use with "Splish! Splash!" on page 7.

Booklet Pages

1. Always have a grown-up watch you while you're in the pool.
2. Walk along the side of the pool; do not run.
3. Look before you jump into the pool.
4. If diving into the pool, make sure you're going into deep water.
5. Do not stay under the diving board.

Name _____

©2000 The Education Center, Inc. • *I Can Make It! I Can Read It!* • *Summer* • TEC3508

Note to the teacher: Use with "Splish! Splash!" on page 7.

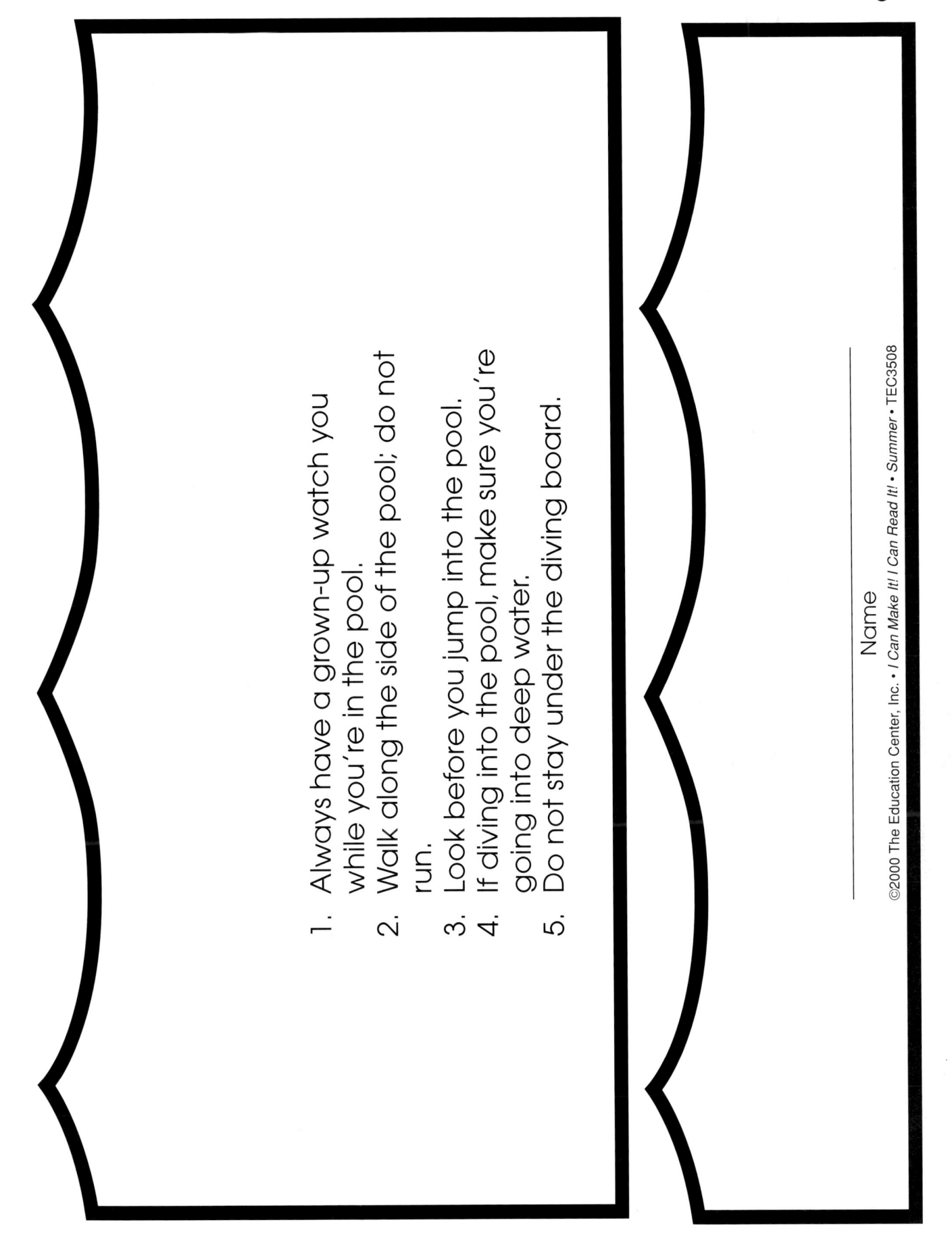

Booklet Page and Patterns

Boy Otter

Girl Otter

Splish! Splash! Who has as much fun in the water as otters? People! To have fun and be safe while you swim, keep these tips in mind.

©2000 The Education Center, Inc. • *I Can Make It! I Can Read It!* • Summer • TEC3508

Note to the teacher: Use with "Splish! Splash!" on page 7.

MMM! MMM! ICE CREAM!

Dish up a tasty reading treat for youngsters and serve this cool booklet! Give each student a copy of pages 12–14. Have him color and cut out his booklet cover and pages. Next, instruct him to stack his pages in numerical order, placing the cover on top. Staple the pages together at the top. Direct him to complete the sentences on each booklet page. Then invite each youngster to read his booklet to the class. Provide time for students to practice reading their booklets with partners. Encourage students to take their booklets home to read to family members. Yum! This booklet looks good enough to eat!

CREATIVE DECORATING OPTIONS

- Glue a red pom-pom to the cover cherry.
- Dab glitter glue on the ice cream to represent sprinkles.

Mmm! Mmm! Ice Cream!

Bud
Name

To extend this booklet-making activity, make a class graph of students' favorite kinds of frozen treats, such as ice-cream sandwiches or Popsicles®. On the chalkboard, list the treats horizontally. Give each student a sticky note and have him write his name on it. In turn, invite each student to post his sticky note in the column of his favorite treat. When all students have had a turn, encourage students to count the number of sticky notes in each column and determine the rankings of the treats.

Booklet Cover and Page

Cover

Mmm! Mmm! Ice Cream!

Name

©2000 The Education Center, Inc.

Page

Vanilla, chocolate, lime, and peach,
All kinds of ice cream are fun to eat!

I like _____ ice cream.

©2000 The Education Center, Inc. • *I Can Make It! I Can Read It!* • Summer • TEC3508

12 **Note to the teacher:** Use with "Mmm! Mmm! Ice Cream!" on page 11.

Booklet Pages

One scoop, two scoops, three scoops, four, I'll eat these and ask for more!

I could eat _____ scoops of ice cream.

2

Eat it in the morning or late at night, Ice cream, ice cream tastes just right.

The best time to eat ice cream is _____.

3

©2000 The Education Center, Inc. • *I Can Make It! I Can Read It!* • Summer • TEC3508

Note to the teacher: Use with "Mmm! Mmm! Ice Cream!" on page 11.

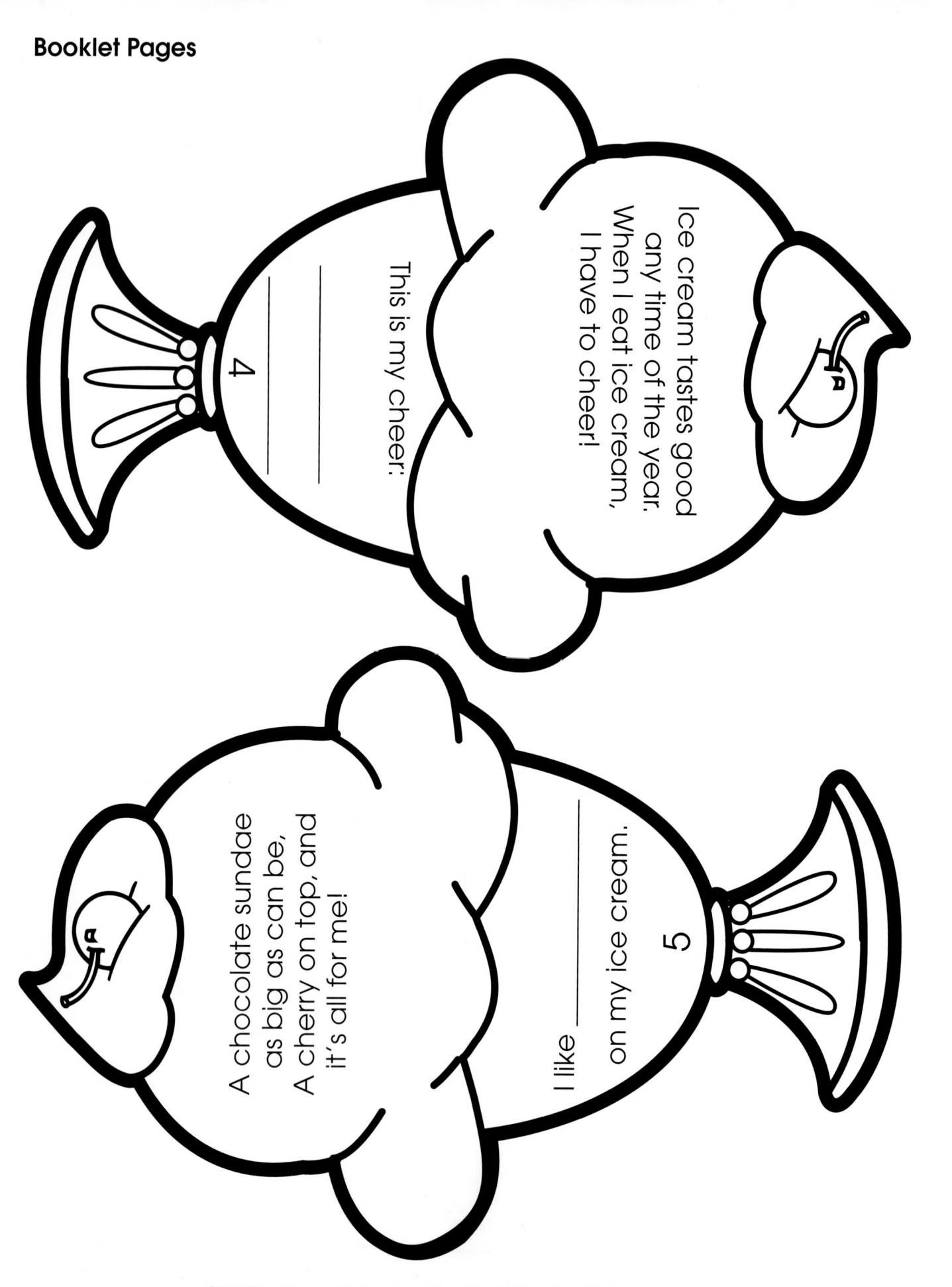

Booklet Pages

Ice cream tastes good
any time of the year.
When I eat ice cream,
I have to cheer!

This is my cheer:
_____
4

A chocolate sundae
as big as can be,
A cherry on top, and
it's all for me!

I like _____
on my ice cream.
5

©2000 The Education Center, Inc. • *I Can Make It! I Can Read It!* • Summer • TEC3508

Note to the teacher: Use with "Mmm! Mmm! Ice Cream!" on page 11.

A TASTE OF WATERMELON

Any way you slice it, youngsters will welcome making and reading this cool watermelon booklet! Give each student a copy of pages 16–18. Have the student color and cut out his booklet pages. Next, instruct him to stack his booklet pages in numerical order, placing the cover on top. Have him staple the pages together at the upper left corner. Then read a completed booklet with students. Provide time for each student to read his booklet with a partner. Encourage students to take their booklets home to read to family members and friends. These tasty booklets are bound to whet students' appetites for reading!

CREATIVE DECORATING OPTIONS

- Glue watermelon seeds to the cover.
- Use red watermelon-scented markers to color the booklet pages.

To extend this booklet-making activity, reinforce math skills with a watermelon party. Invite students to watch as you cut up a large watermelon into equal portions. Cut the watermelon into halves, quarters, and eighths as you explain the concepts of fractions accordingly. Next, give each child a piece of watermelon and instruct him to estimate how many seeds are in it. Once he has eaten his watermelon, have him count the number of seeds that remain and compare it to his guess. What a refreshing way to practice math skills!

Booklet Cover and Page

Cover

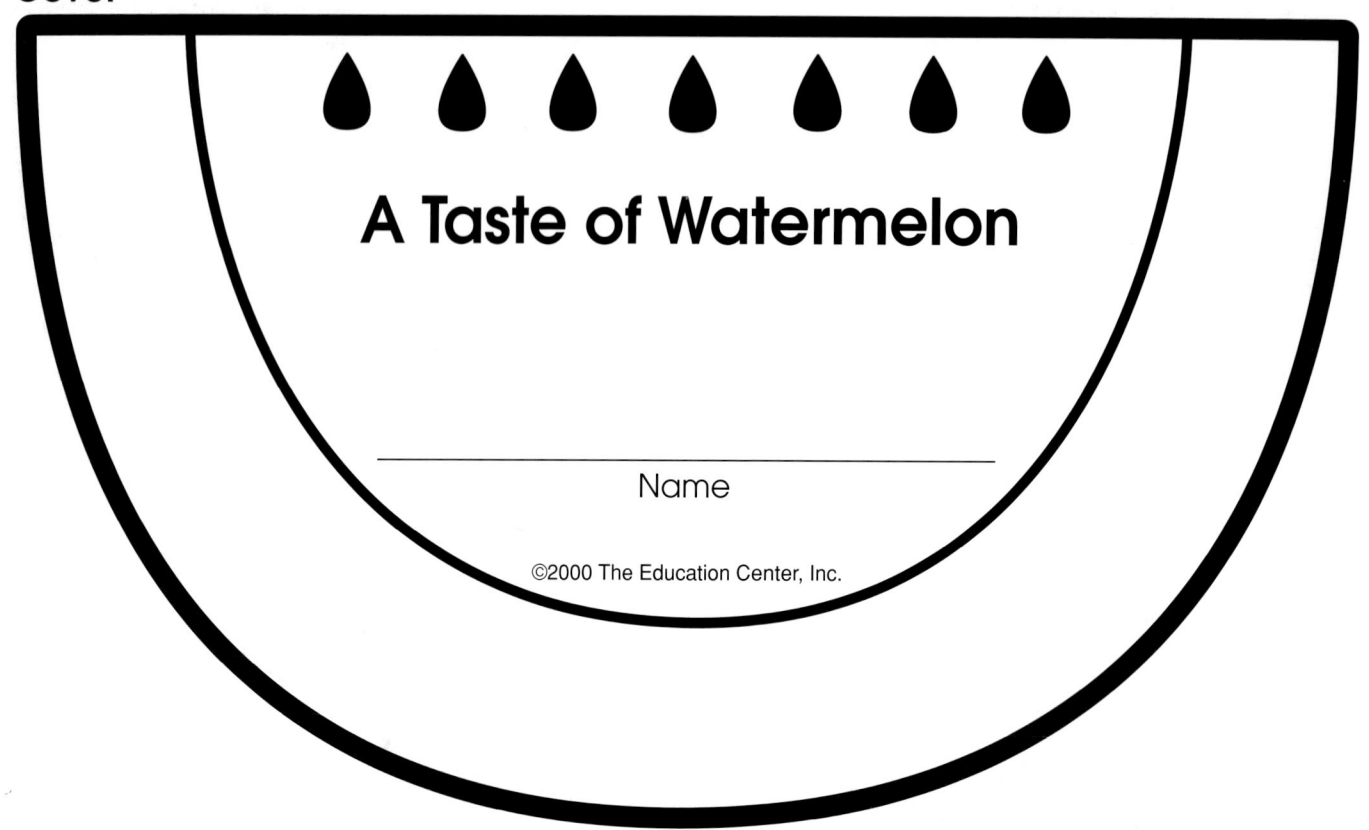

A Taste of Watermelon

Name

©2000 The Education Center, Inc.

Page

When I'm feeling hungry and
I want something quick,
I cut a slice of watermelon,
juicy and thick.

1

©2000 The Education Center, Inc. • I Can Make It! I Can Read It! • Summer • TEC3508

Note to the teacher: Use with "A Taste of Watermelon" on page 15.

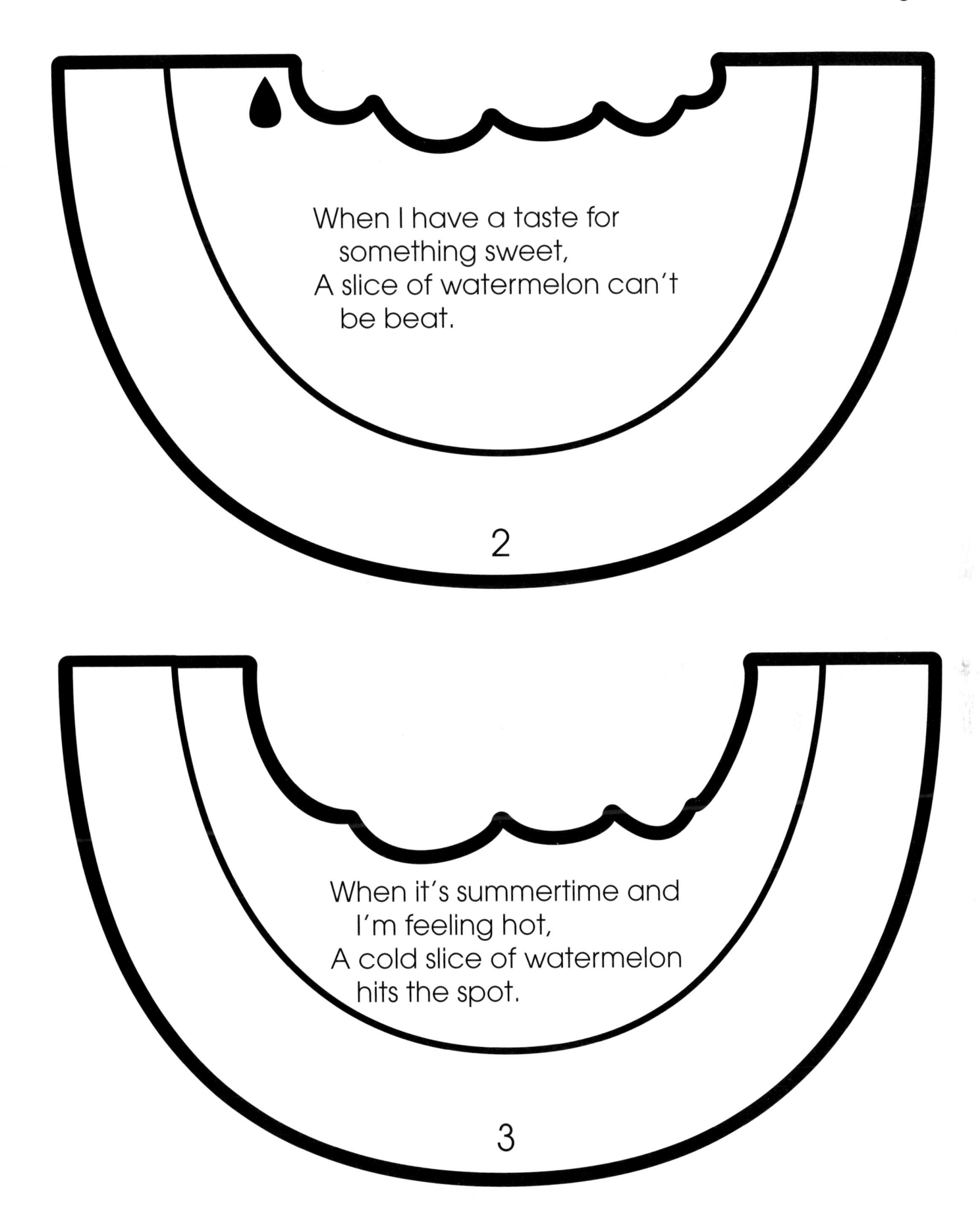

Booklet Pages

When I have a taste for something sweet,
A slice of watermelon can't be beat.

2

When it's summertime and I'm feeling hot,
A cold slice of watermelon hits the spot.

3

©2000 The Education Center, Inc. • *I Can Make It! I Can Read It!* • Summer • TEC3508

Note to the teacher: Use with "A Taste of Watermelon" on page 15.

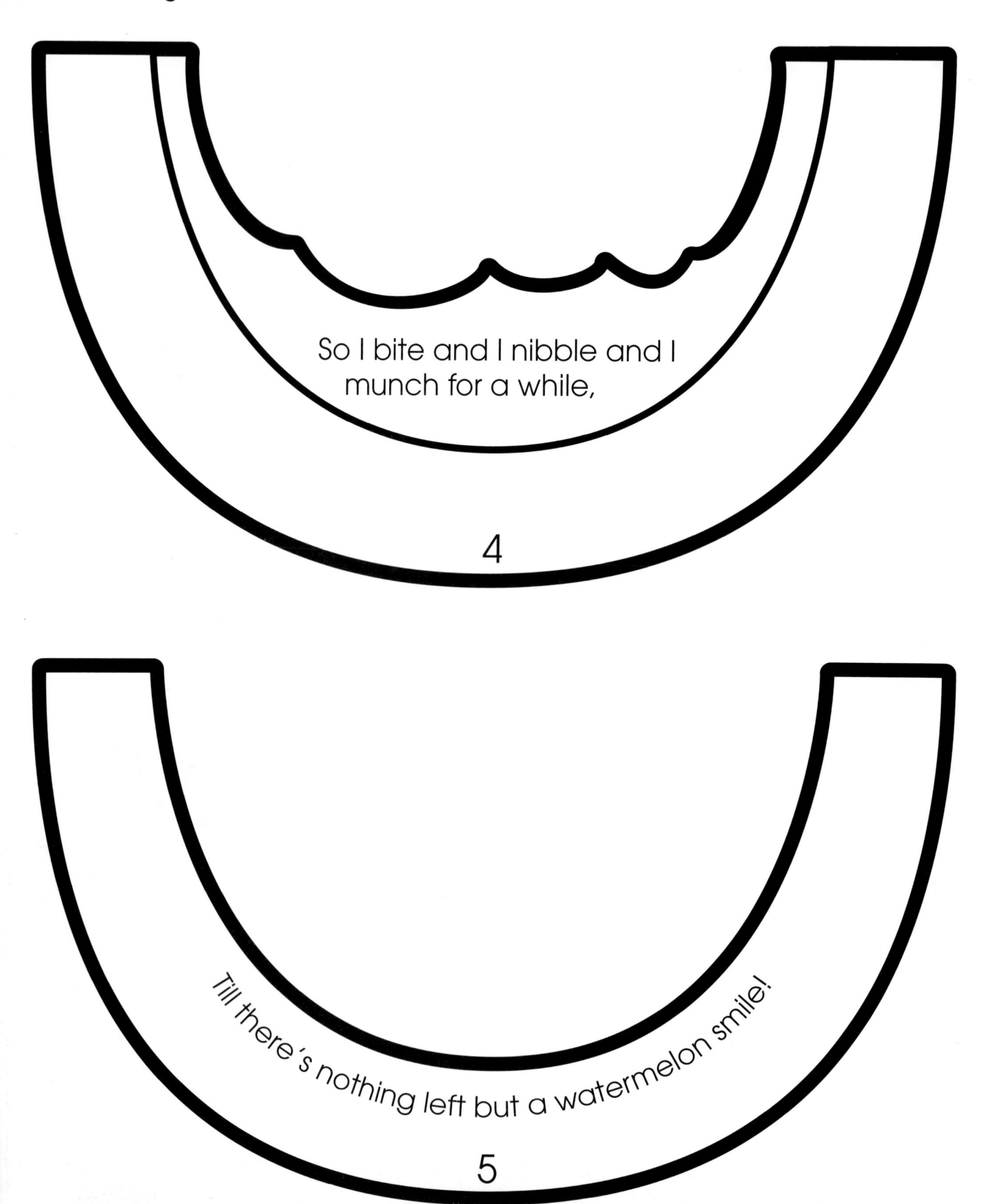

Booklet Pages

So I bite and I nibble and I munch for a while,

4

Till there's nothing left but a watermelon smile!

5

FAMILY FUN

Summer fun is all in the family with this flip booklet! Give each student a copy of pages 20–24. Have the student color her top pages, bottom pages, and cover illustrations and then cut them out along the bold outer lines. Direct her to cut slits along the bold lines of her top pages. Next, have her glue the bottom pages together where indicated. Then instruct her to glue the top pages to the bottom pages where indicated. When the glue is dry, have her fold her booklet in half widthwise and then glue the illustrations to the appropriate covers as shown. Read a completed booklet with students. Provide time for students to practice reading their booklets with one another. Invite youngsters to take their booklets home to share with family members.

CREATIVE DECORATING OPTIONS

- After coloring the top pages with crayons, paint a blue watercolor wash over them.
- Glue sand around the edges of the front cover.

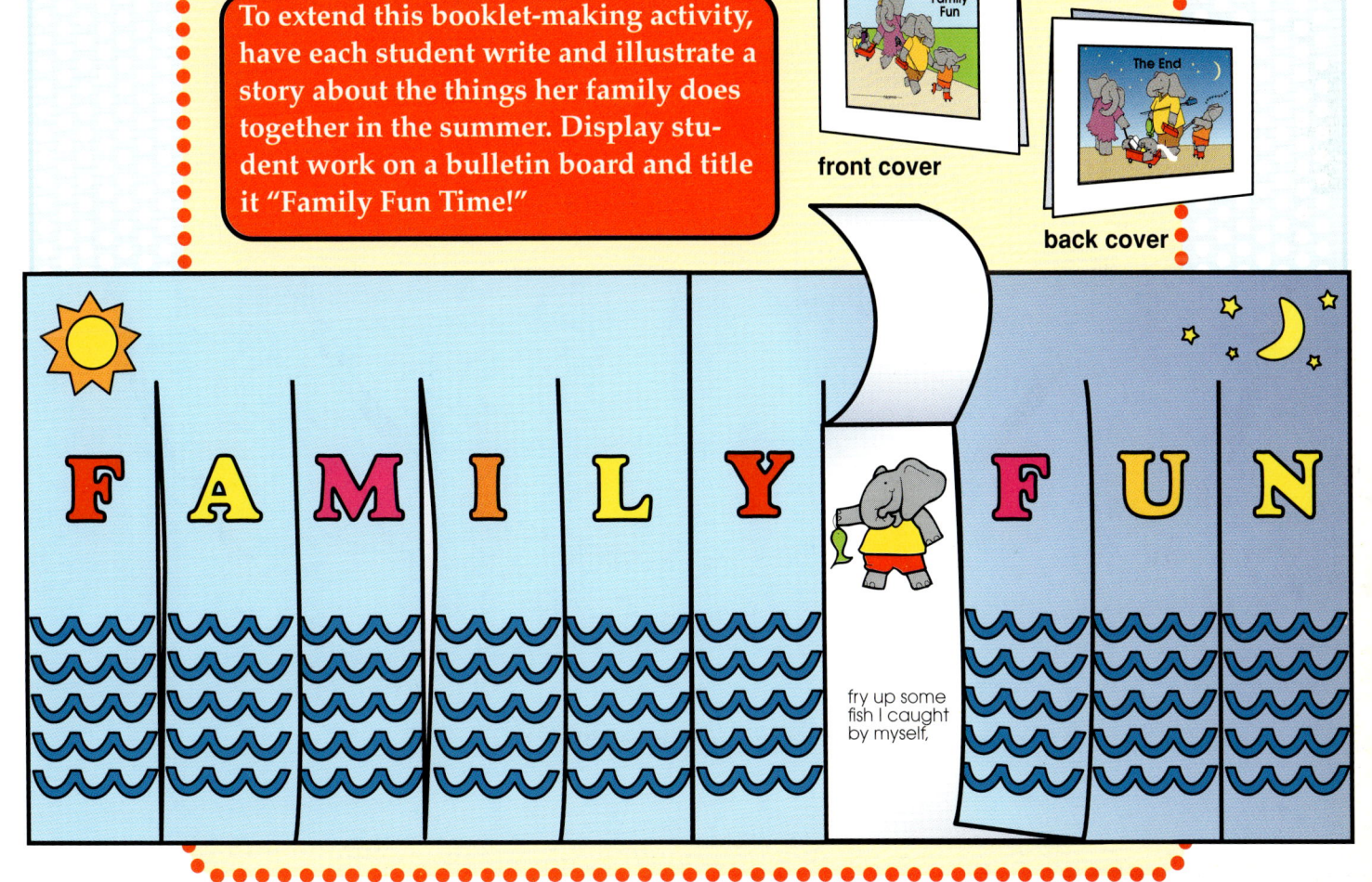

To extend this booklet-making activity, have each student write and illustrate a story about the things her family does together in the summer. Display student work on a bulletin board and title it "Family Fun Time!"

front cover

back cover

F A M I L Y F U N

fry up some fish I caught by myself,

Booklet Pattern

Top Page 1

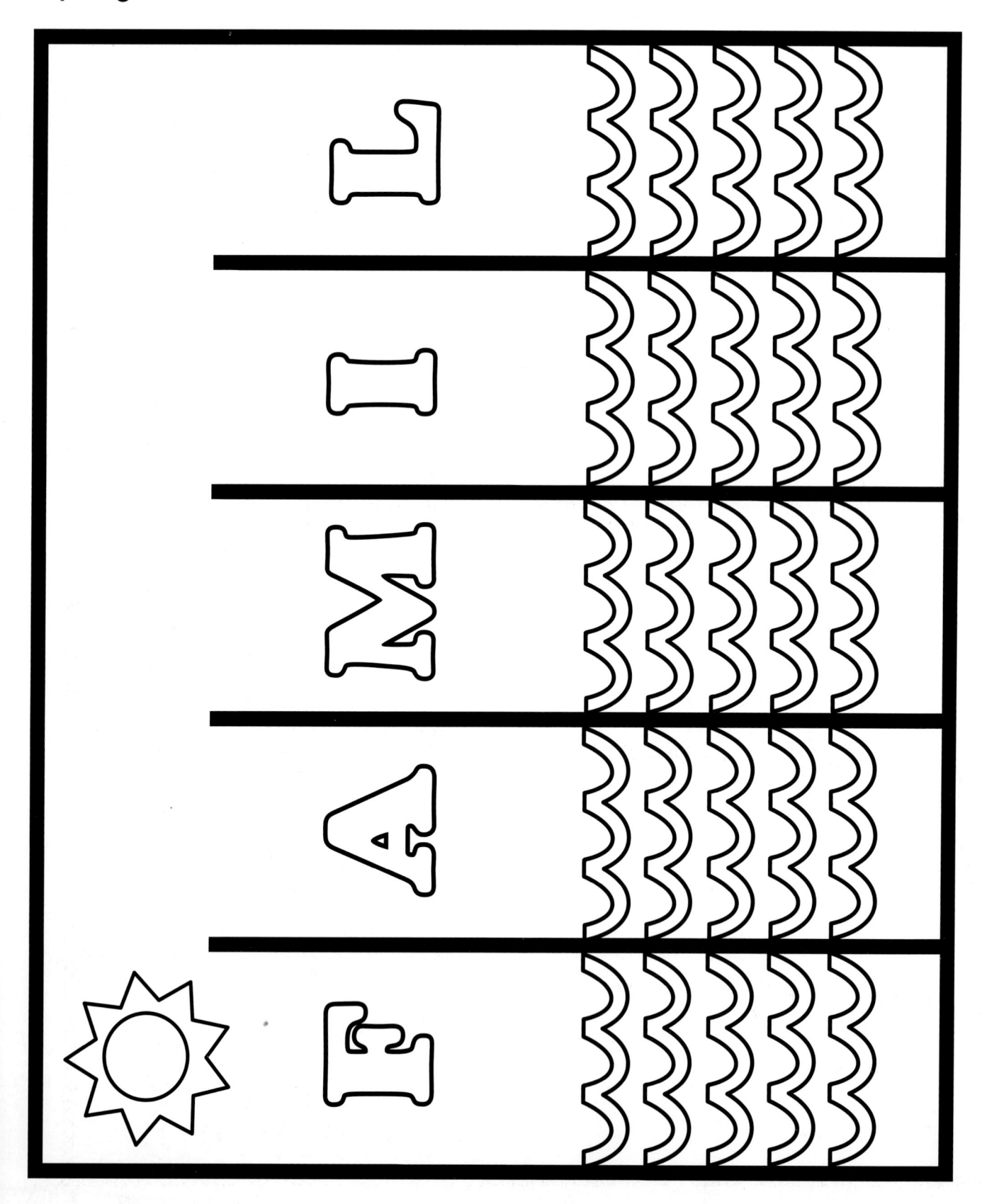

©2000 The Education Center, Inc. • *I Can Make It! I Can Read It!* • *Summer* • TEC3508

20 **Note to the teacher:** Use with "Family Fun" on page 19.

Booklet Pattern

Top Page 2

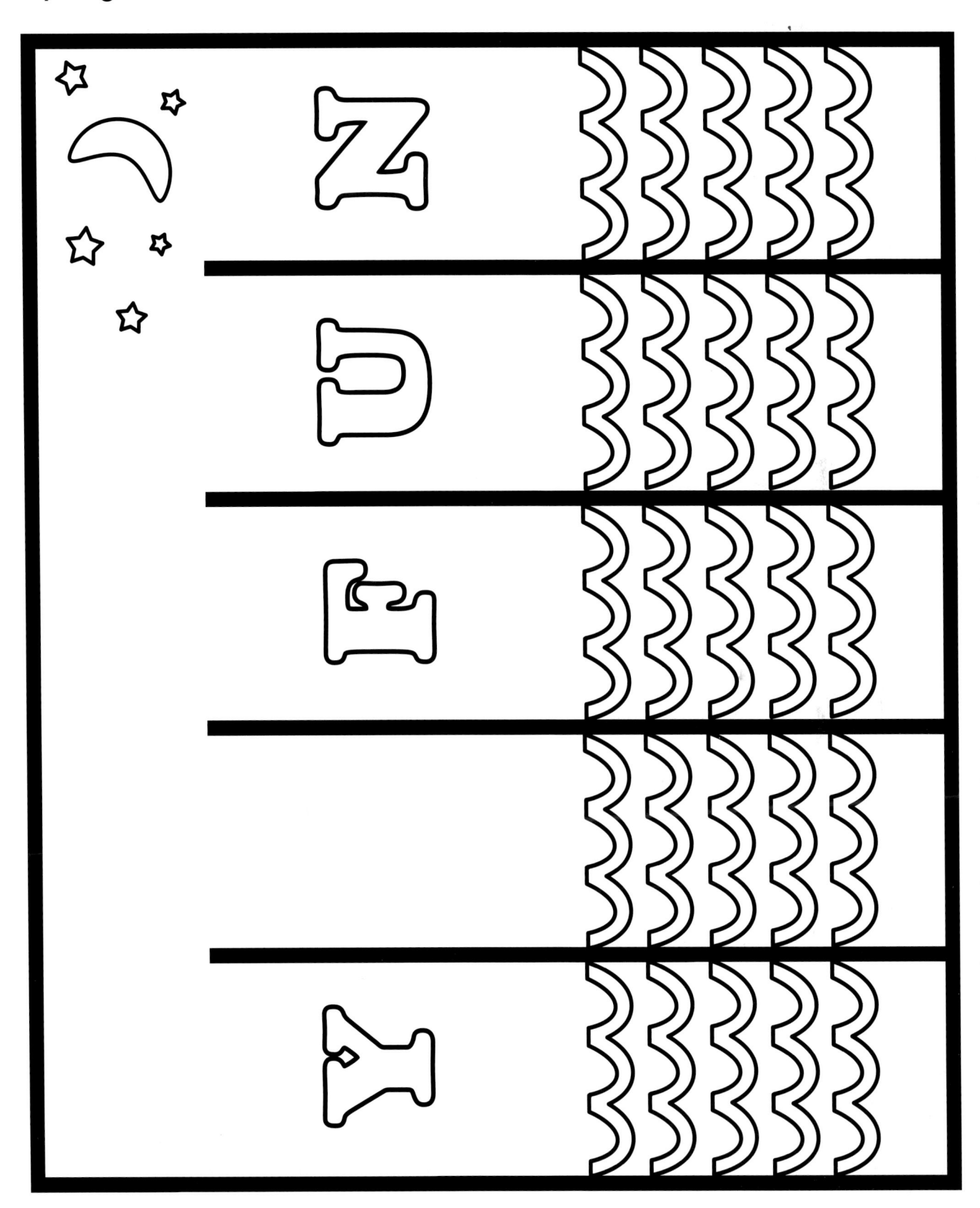

©2000 The Education Center, Inc. • *I Can Make It! I Can Read It!* • Summer • TEC3508

Note to the teacher: Use with "Family Fun" on page 19.

21

Bottom Page 1

Summer is the best time for me to play outside with my family.

We pedal down the path that leads through the park,

skate down the sidewalk until it grows dark,

swim in the sea and get sand in our shoes,

bring books to the beach and read one or two,

Glue top page 1 here.

©2000 The Education Center, Inc. • I Can Make It! I Can Read It! • Summer • TEC3508

22 **Note to the teacher:** Use with "Family Fun" on page 19.

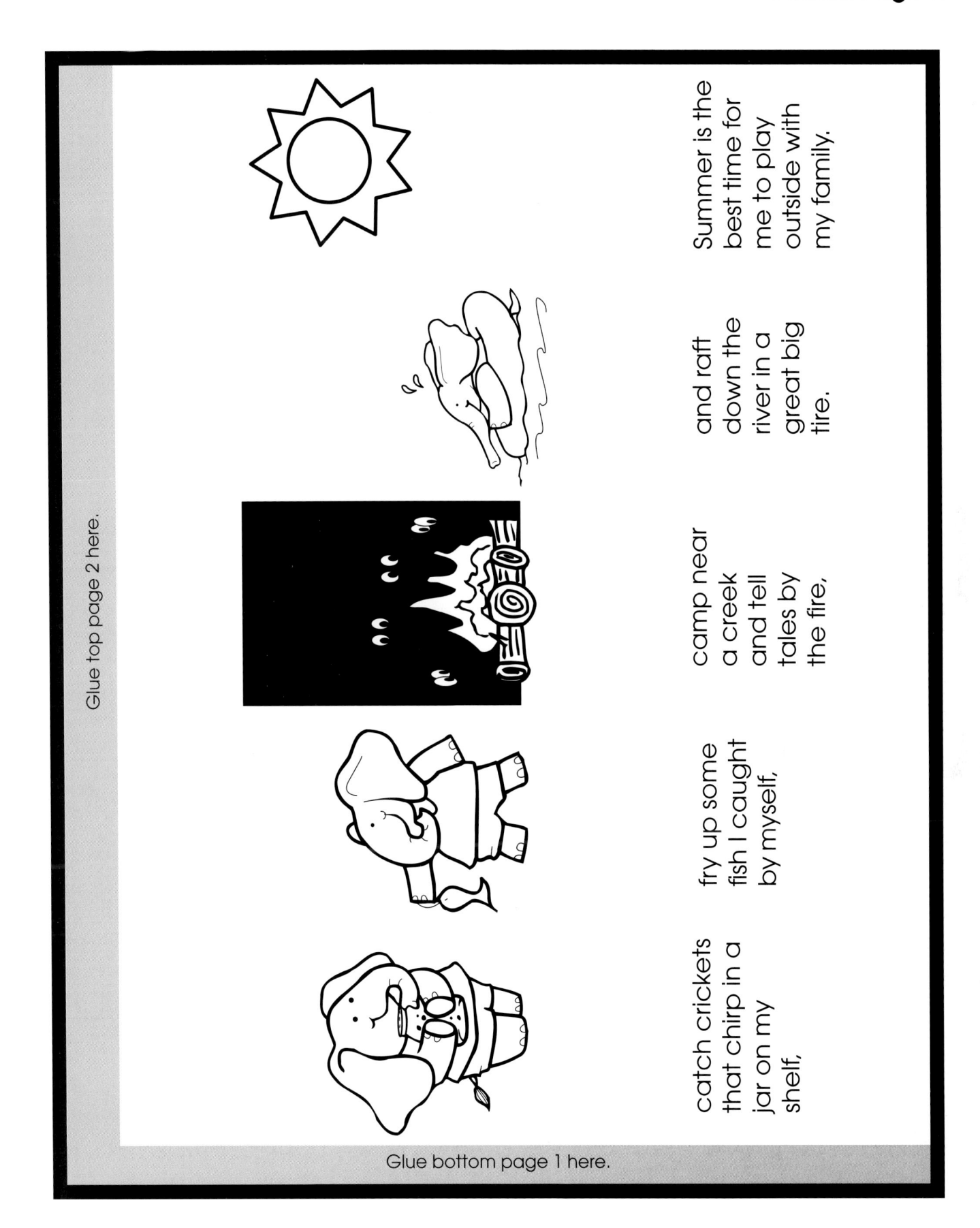

Bottom Page 2

Glue top page 2 here.

catch crickets that chirp in a jar on my shelf,

fry up some fish I caught by myself,

camp near a creek and tell tales by the fire,

and raft down the river in a great big tire.

Summer is the best time for me to play outside with my family.

Glue bottom page 1 here.

©2000 The Education Center, Inc. • *I Can Make It! I Can Read It!* • Summer • TEC3508

Note to the teacher: Use with "Family Fun" on page 19.

Cover Illustrations
Front Cover

Family Fun

Name

©2000 The Education Center, Inc. • *I Can Make It! I Can Read It!* • Summer • TEC3508

Back Cover

The End

©2000 The Education Center, Inc. • *I Can Make It! I Can Read It!* • Summer • TEC3508

24 **Note to the teacher:** Use with "Family Fun" on page 19.

WHAT MIGHT YOU SEE?

What are some sights you might see on the Fourth of July in the USA? Find out when you read this banner booklet! Give each student a blue construction paper copy of page 26, a red construction paper copy of page 27, white copies of pages 28–30, and a 25" length of red, white, or blue yarn. Have each student cut out his booklet backing, patterns, cover, and pages on the bold outer lines. Next, direct him to glue the red stripes and then the white stripes to the backing as shown. Instruct him to fold back the backing where indicated, center the yarn in the crease of the fold (see the illustration), and then glue down the fold. Have him tie the ends of the yarn together. Allow the glue to dry. Next, instruct him to stack his booklet pages in numerical order, placing the cover on top. Have him staple the booklet to the backing where indicated and glue on the stars. Then read a completed booklet with students. Provide time for each student to practice reading with a buddy before he takes his booklet home to read to family members. Happy birthday, USA!

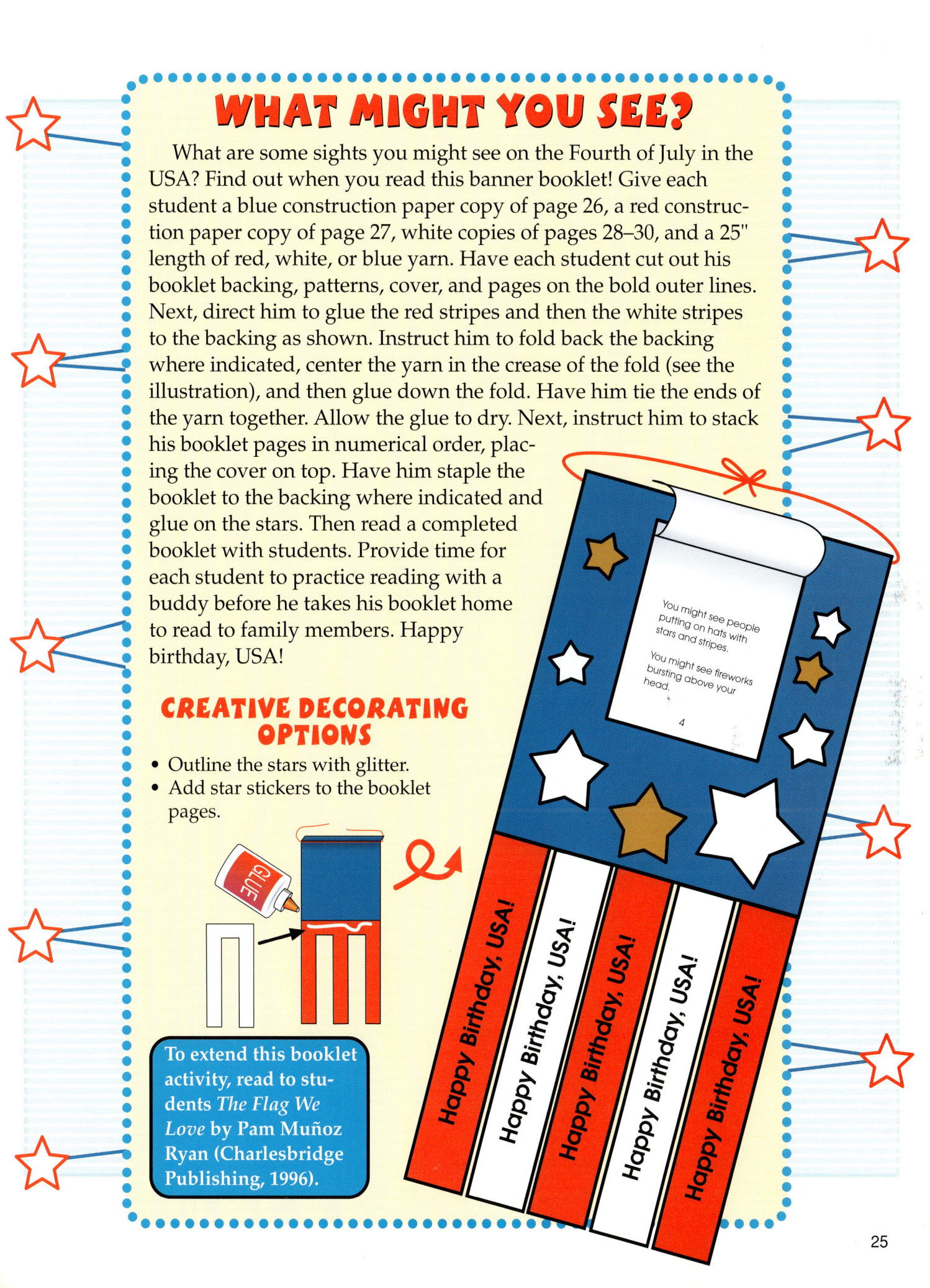

CREATIVE DECORATING OPTIONS

- Outline the stars with glitter.
- Add star stickers to the booklet pages.

To extend this booklet activity, read to students *The Flag We Love* by Pam Muñoz Ryan (Charlesbridge Publishing, 1996).

Booklet Backing

Fold.

Staple the booklet pages here.

Red Stripes

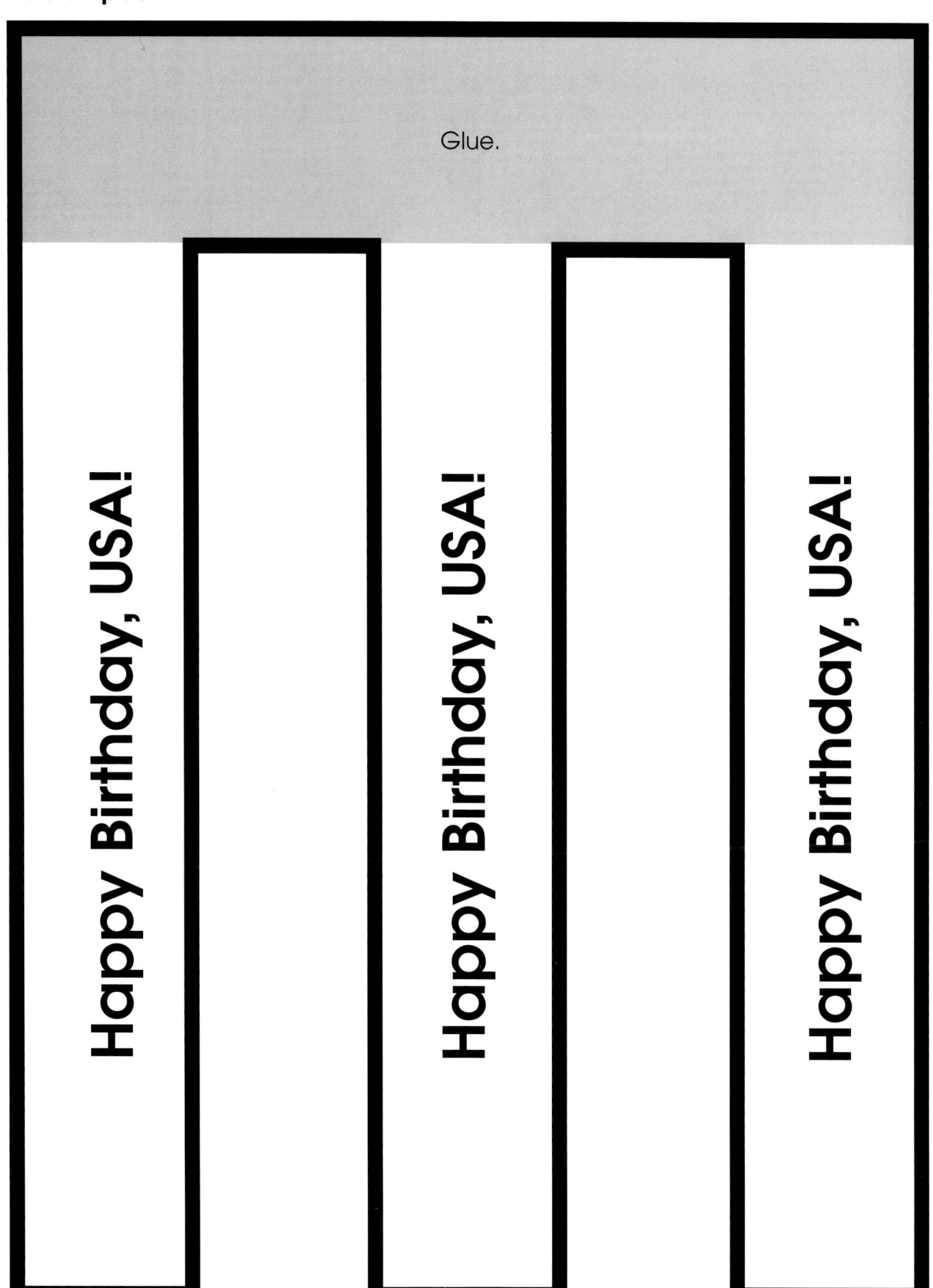

Booklet Pattern

Glue.

Happy Birthday, USA!

Happy Birthday, USA!

Happy Birthday, USA!

©2000 The Education Center, Inc. • *I Can Make It! I Can Read It!* • *Summer* • TEC3508

Note to the teacher: Use with "What Might You See?" on page 25.

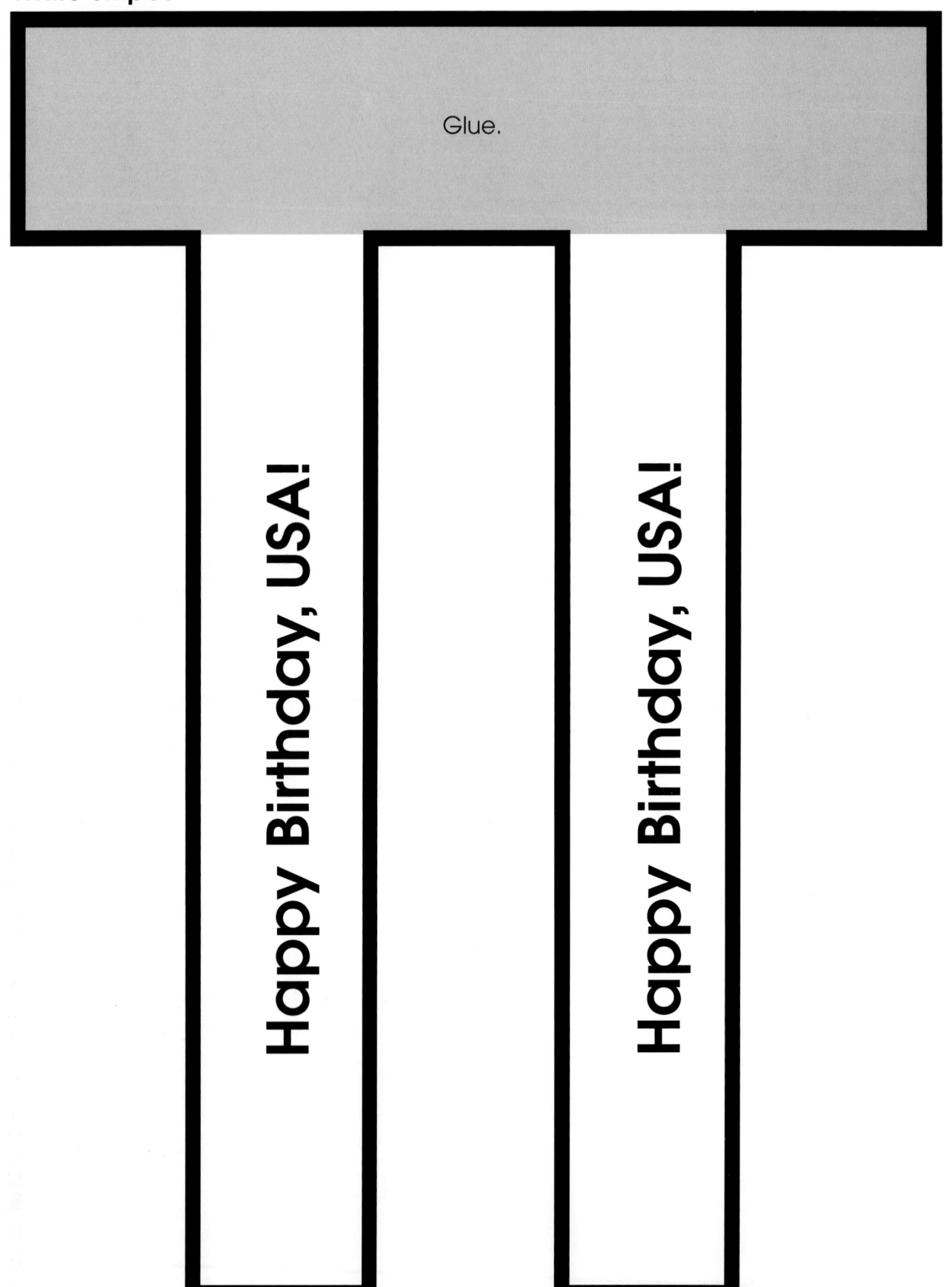

Booklet Pattern

White Stripes

Glue.

Happy Birthday, USA!

Happy Birthday, USA!

©2000 The Education Center, Inc. • *I Can Make It! I Can Read It!* • *Summer* • TEC3508

Note to the teacher: Use with "What Might You See?" on page 25.

Booklet Patterns, Cover, and Page

Stars

Cover

What Might You See?

_____
Name

©2000 The Education Center, Inc.

Page

The Fourth of July is a big day for the people of the USA. It is the USA's birthday!

What might you see on the Fourth of July?

1

©2000 The Education Center, Inc. • *I Can Make It! I Can Read It!* • Summer • TEC3508

Note to the teacher: Use with "What Might You See?" on page 25.

Booklet Pages

You might see children waving flags over their heads.

You might see bands marching in a parade.

2

You might see families having picnics in the park.

You might see men wearing ties of red, white, and blue.

3

You might see people putting on hats with stars and stripes.

You might see fireworks bursting above your head.

4

What might you see on the Fourth of July? People having fun!

Happy birthday to the United States of America!

5

OH, GOODY! IT'S A PICNIC!

Give youngsters a basketful of reading with this interactive picnic booklet! Give each student a brown construction paper copy of page 32, a white copy of pages 33–34, and a brad. Have the student color her booklet pages and ants. Then instruct her to cut out the booklet pages and patterns along the bold outer lines. Have her punch a hole in the handle and basket front where indicated. Direct her to insert the brad through the handle and basket front as shown. Next, instruct her to glue the basket back to the basket front where indicated and the ants to the front as shown. Allow the glue to dry. Then read the booklet pages with students. Stack the pages, rotate the handle to one side, and place the pages in the basket. Provide time for students to practice reading their completed booklets with one another. Encourage students to take their booklets home to read to family members and friends. What's in the basket? A reading feast!

CREATIVE DECORATING OPTION
- Tuck a tissue in the basket to represent a cloth cover.

To extend this activity, use the booklet pages to reinforce classification skills. Tell students they are going to pack a few items for a picnic. Then announce a classification, such as foods, and have each student pack her basket with the appropriate booklet pages. When students have made their choices, have a student tell the class what she chose and why. Accept reasonable responses. Then repeat the activity by announcing a different classification.

Booklet Patterns

Basket Front

Name

©2000 The Education Center, Inc.

What's packed inside the picnic basket?

Handle

Oh, Goody! It's a Picnic!

Basket Back

Glue.

©2000 The Education Center, Inc. • *I Can Make It! I Can Read It!* • *Summer* • TEC3508

Note to the teacher: Use with "Oh, Goody! It's a Picnic!" on page 31.

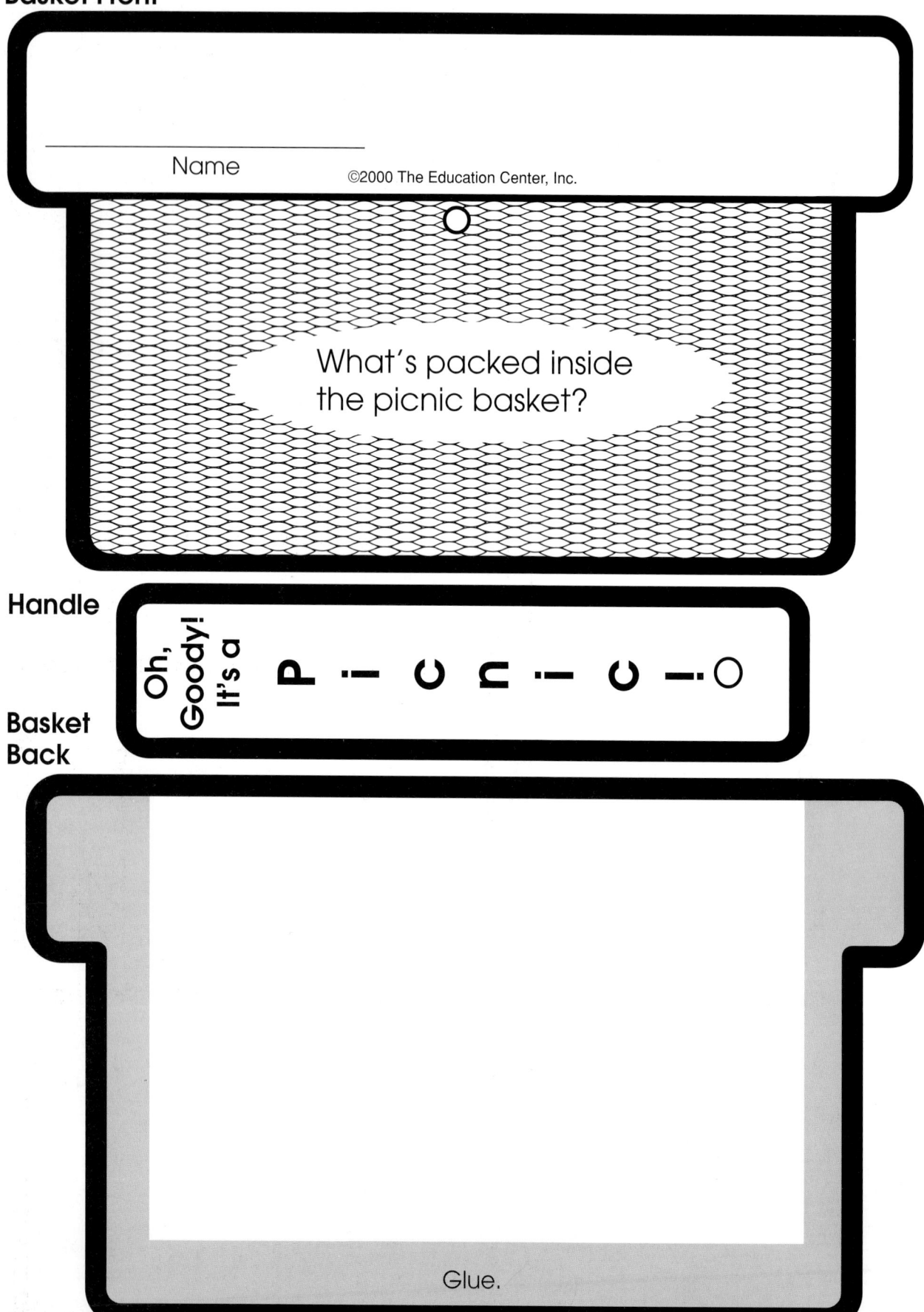

Booklet Patterns and Pages

Ants

Pages

There are cold drinks.

There is a yummy chocolate cake.

There is fried chicken.

There are watermelon slices.

There are lots of bags of chips.

There is a yellow Frisbee®.

©2000 The Education Center, Inc. • *I Can Make It! I Can Read It!* • *Summer* • TEC3508

Note to the teacher: Use with "Oh, Goody! It's a Picnic!" on page 31.

Booklet Pages

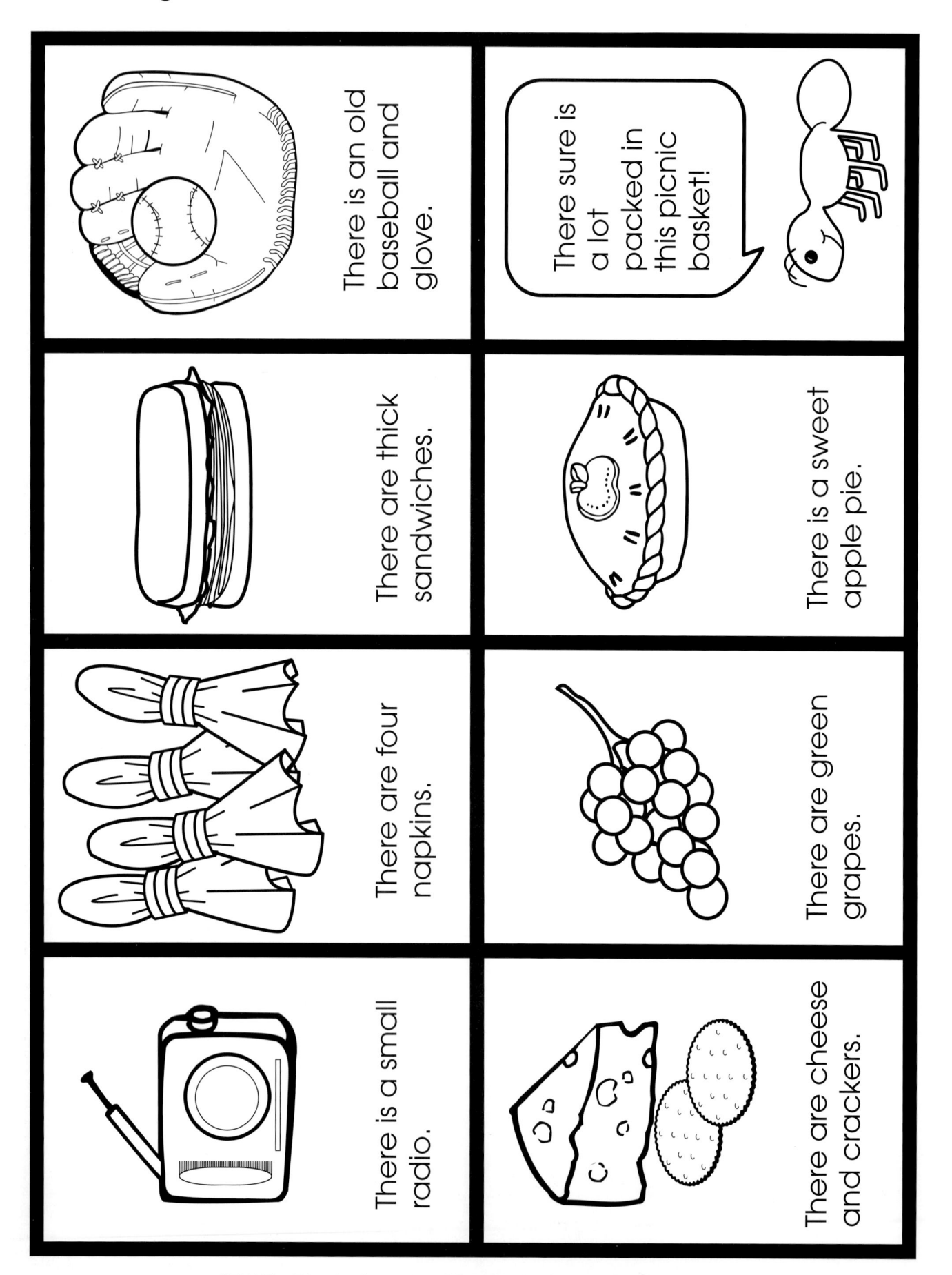

There is an old baseball and glove.

There sure is a lot packed in this picnic basket!

There are thick sandwiches.

There is a sweet apple pie.

There are four napkins.

There are green grapes.

There is a small radio.

There are cheese and crackers.

©2000 The Education Center, Inc. • *I Can Make It! I Can Read It!* • Summer • TEC3508

34 **Note to the teacher:** Use with "Oh, Goody! It's a Picnic!" on page 31.

A-CAMPING WE WILL GO!

Get your youngsters geared up for reading with this camping shape book! Give each student a copy of pages 36–38. Have the student color his booklet backing. (Remind students to color lightly over the text so the booklet can be read.) Next, instruct the student to cut out his booklet backing and pages along the bold outer lines. Direct him to stack his pages in numerical order, placing the cover on top. Have him align the stacked pages with booklet page 4 and staple them together at the top. Then read a completed booklet with students. Provide time for students to practice reading together. Encourage students to take their booklets home to read to family members.

CREATIVE DECORATING OPTION

- Glue the backing to a 9" x 12" sheet of dark blue construction paper. Apply star stickers to the construction paper to create a night scene.

To extend this booklet-making activity, share the antics of two cubs who explore a family's campsite. Read aloud *Where Are the Bears?* by Kay Winters (Bantam Doubleday Dell Publishing Group, Inc.,; 1998).

A-camping We Will Go!

Richard
Name

Booklet Cover and Page

Cover

A-camping We Will Go!

Name

©2000 The Education Center, Inc. • *I Can Make It! I Can Read It!* • *Summer* • TEC3508

Page

I'm one bear that loves campers! Every summer, I stand behind a tree and watch campers set up.

1

Booklet Pages

They hop out of their cars. They set up tents and sleeping bags. They pull out bikes and balls. They take out games and jump ropes. They set out puzzles and books. They set up coolers and radios. They open bags of chips and cookies.

2

The smell of chips and cookies makes my stomach growl. The campers look up in surprise. "A-A-A-A-H-H-H-H!" they scream.

3

©2000 The Education Center, Inc. • *I Can Make It! I Can Read It!* • Summer • TEC3508

Note to the teacher: Use with "A-camping We Will Go!" on page 35.

Booklet Backing

They stuff the tents and sleeping bags into their cars. They grab the bikes and balls. They snatch up the games, jump ropes, puzzles, and books. They grab the coolers and radios. They are gone in a flash, leaving behind the bags of chips and cookies.

Mmmm, I do love campers!

4

©2000 The Education Center, Inc. • *I Can Make It! I Can Read It!* • Summer • TEC3508

Note to the teacher: Use with "A-camping We Will Go!" on page 35.

LET'S GO ON VACATION!

Here's a vacation booklet that's packed with fun! Give each student a copy of pages 40–44. Have the student cut out her booklet pages along the bold outer lines. Then read the booklet pages with students. Instruct the student to draw the clothes Dad would pack at the top of booklet page 2 and those Mom would pack at the top of booklet page 3. For booklet pages 4 and 5, have her answer the questions and illustrate them at the top of the page. Next, instruct her to stack her pages in numerical order and staple them at the top. Then invite each student to read her booklet and show her illustrations to the class. Encourage students to take their booklets home to share with family members and friends.

CREATIVE DECORATING OPTIONS

- Cut out pictures of clothing from discarded catalogs or magazines and glue them to the tops of the appropriate booklet pages.
- Cut out pictures from travel brochures and glue them to the appropriate pages.

To extend this booklet-making activity, read to students *Arthur's Family Vacation* by Marc Brown (Little, Brown and Company; 1993).

Mom says she would like to go someplace warm so that we can sit by the pool.

Booklet Page

Let's Go on Vacation!

_____
Name

©2000 The Education Center, Inc. • *I Can Make It! I Can Read It!* • *Summer* • TEC3508

It's vacation time.
Time to get away.
Where will we go?
Where will we stay?

1

©2000 The Education Center, Inc. • *I Can Make It! I Can Read It!* • *Summer* • TEC3508

Note to the teacher: Use with "Let's Go on Vacation!" on page 39.

Dad says he would like to go to the mountains, where the air is nice and cool.

2

Booklet Page

Mom says she would like to go someplace warm so that we can sit by the pool.

3

Note to the teacher: Use with "Let's Go on Vacation!" on page 39.

Booklet Page

Where should we go?

4

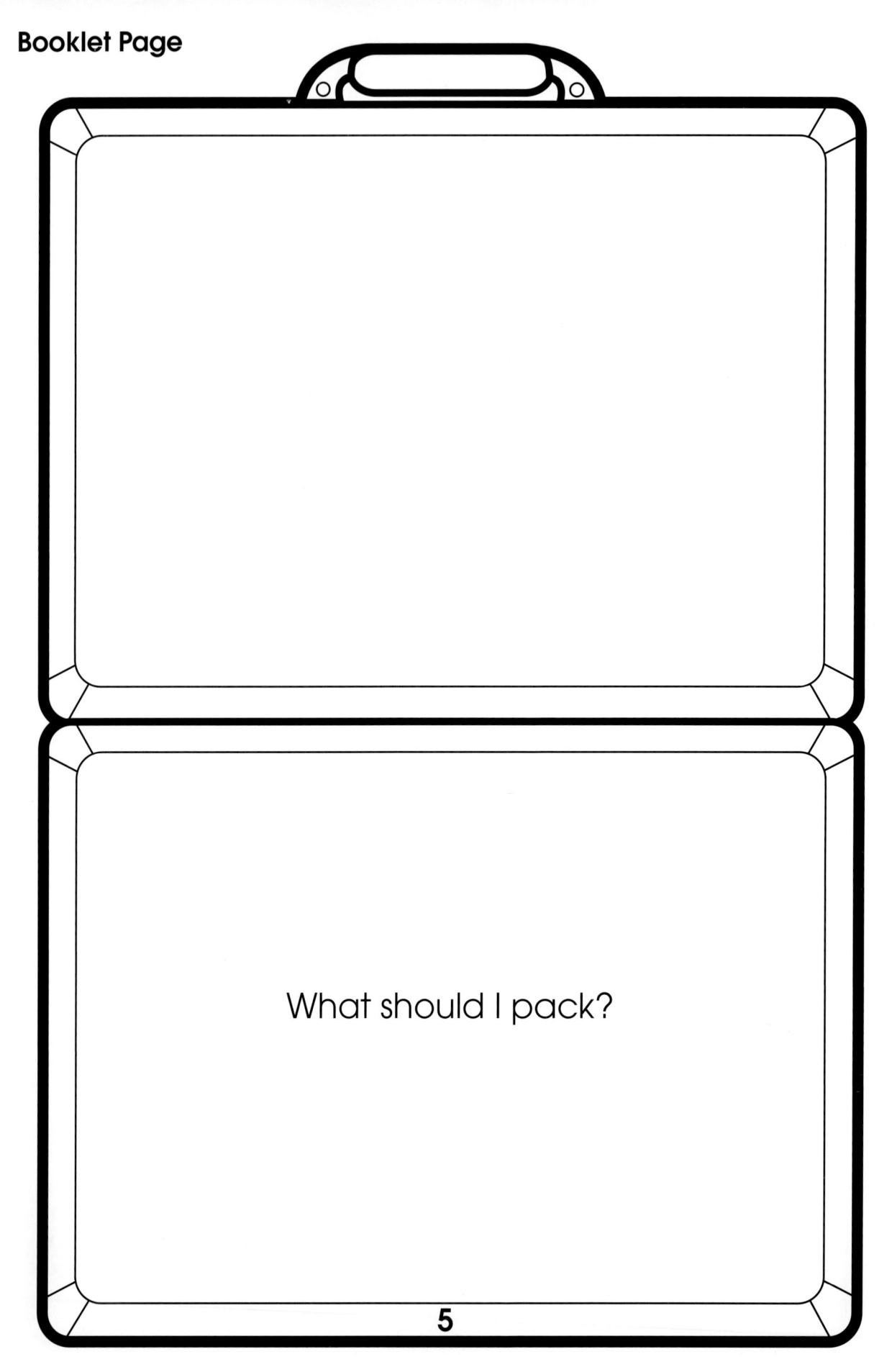

Booklet Page

What should I pack?

5

©2000 The Education Center, Inc. • *I Can Make It! I Can Read It!* • Summer • TEC3508

Note to the teacher: Use with "Let's Go on Vacation!" on page 39.

BUTTERFLY OR MOTH?

Youngsters will be in a flutter over reading with this informative booklet about butterflies and moths! Give each student construction paper copy of page 46 and white copies of pages 47–50. If desired, have the student color her cover and illustrations. Then instruct her to cut out the booklet cover and pages on the bold outer lines. Have her fold her booklet cover in half. Next, direct her to stack her pages in numerical order, keeping the matching pages face-to-face as shown. Place the stacked pages inside the folded cover and staple them together at the left. Instruct her to lightly glue the blank pages together. Then read a completed booklet with students. Provide time for students to practice reading their booklets with partners. Encourage students to take their booklets home to read to family members and friends.

CREATIVE DECORATING OPTIONS

- Glue pipe cleaners to the cover to represent antennae. (Remind students to leave the pipe cleaners straight for a moth or curl the tips for a butterfly.)
- Add sequins to the cover.

To extend this booklet-making activity, read to students Bobbie Kalman's *Butterflies and Moths* (Crabtree Publishing Company, 1994).

Booklet Cover

Butterfly or Moth?

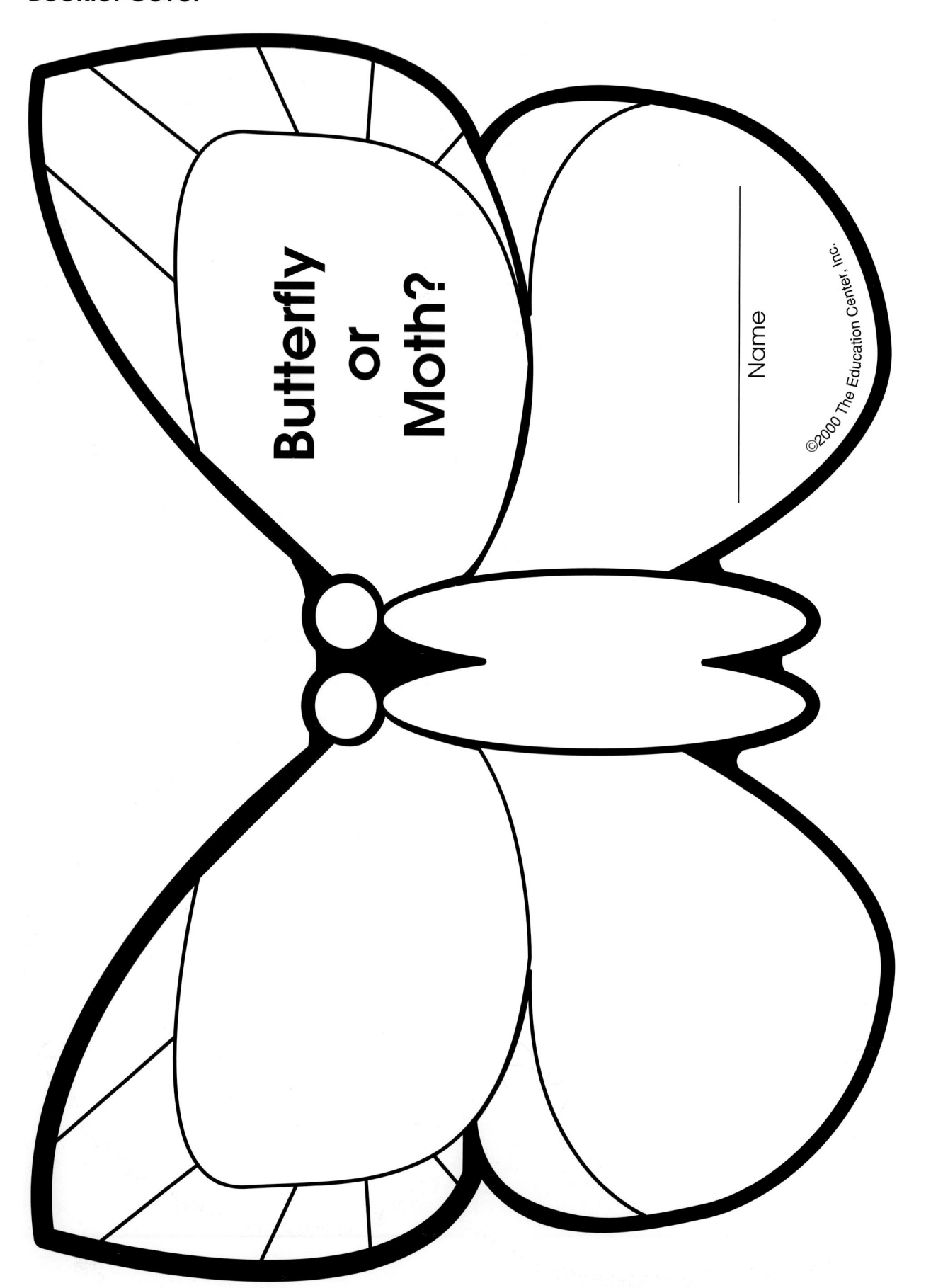

Name _____

©2000 The Education Center, Inc.

©2000 The Education Center, Inc. • *I Can Make It! I Can Read It!* • Summer • TEC3508

Note to the teacher: Use with "Butterfly or Moth?" on page 45.

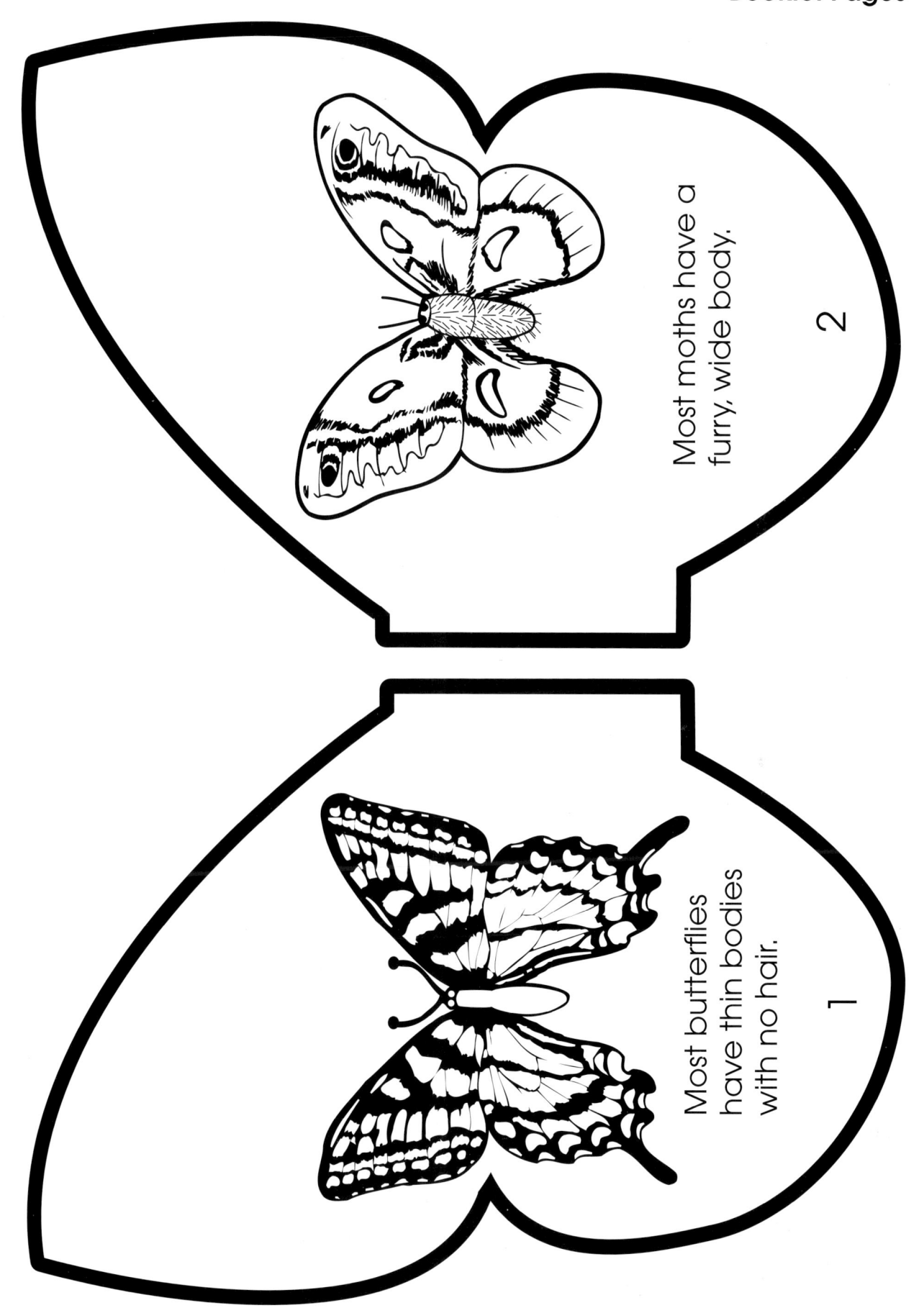

Booklet Pages

Most moths have a furry, wide body.

2

Most butterflies have thin bodies with no hair.

1

©2000 The Education Center, Inc. • *I Can Make It! I Can Read It!* • Summer • TEC3508

Note to the teacher: Use with "Butterfly or Moth?" on page 45.

Booklet Pages

Most moths keep their wings down when they are resting.

4

Most butterflies keep their wings up when they are resting.

3

Note to the teacher: Use with "Butterfly or Moth?" on page 45.

Booklet Pages

Most moths do not have knobs at the ends of their antennae.

6

Most butterflies have knobs at the ends of their antennae.

5

©2000 The Education Center, Inc. • *I Can Make It! I Can Read It!* • *Summer* • TEC3508

Note to the teacher: Use with "Butterfly or Moth?" on page 45.

Booklet Pages

Most moths fly in the nighttime.

8

Most butterflies fly in the daytime.

7

©2000 The Education Center, Inc. • *I Can Make It! I Can Read It!* • *Summer* • TEC3508

Note to the teacher: Use with "Butterfly or Moth?" on page 45.

COBRAS-S-S!

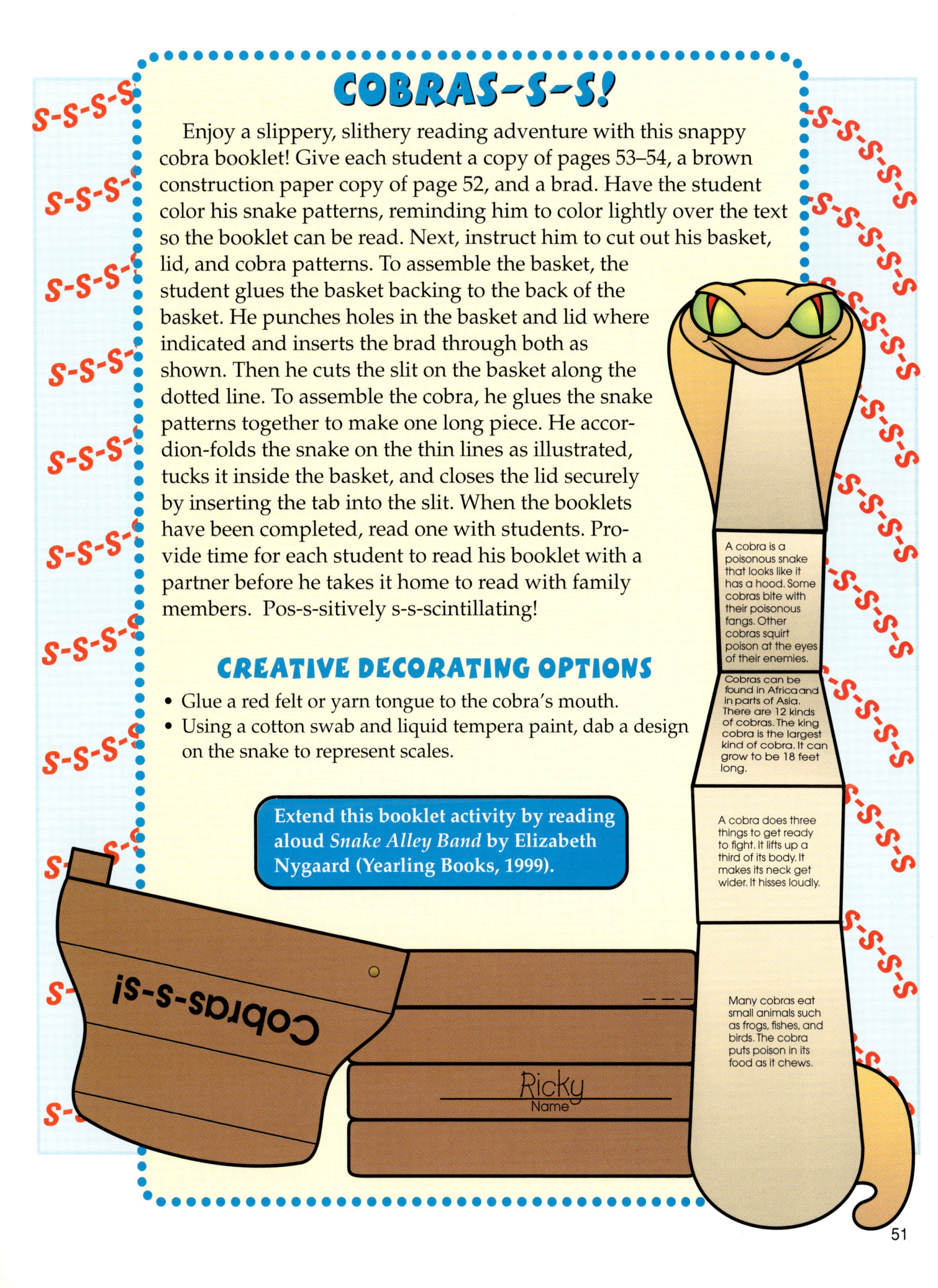

Enjoy a slippery, slithery reading adventure with this snappy cobra booklet! Give each student a copy of pages 53–54, a brown construction paper copy of page 52, and a brad. Have the student color his snake patterns, reminding him to color lightly over the text so the booklet can be read. Next, instruct him to cut out his basket, lid, and cobra patterns. To assemble the basket, the student glues the basket backing to the back of the basket. He punches holes in the basket and lid where indicated and inserts the brad through both as shown. Then he cuts the slit on the basket along the dotted line. To assemble the cobra, he glues the snake patterns together to make one long piece. He accordion-folds the snake on the thin lines as illustrated, tucks it inside the basket, and closes the lid securely by inserting the tab into the slit. When the booklets have been completed, read one with students. Provide time for each student to read his booklet with a partner before he takes it home to read with family members. Pos-s-sitively s-s-scintillating!

CREATIVE DECORATING OPTIONS

- Glue a red felt or yarn tongue to the cobra's mouth.
- Using a cotton swab and liquid tempera paint, dab a design on the snake to represent scales.

Extend this booklet activity by reading aloud *Snake Alley Band* by Elizabeth Nygaard (Yearling Books, 1999).

A cobra is a poisonous snake that looks like it has a hood. Some cobras bite with their poisonous fangs. Other cobras squirt poison at the eyes of their enemies.

Cobras can be found in Africa and in parts of Asia. There are 12 kinds of cobras. The king cobra is the largest kind of cobra. It can grow to be 18 feet long.

A cobra does three things to get ready to fight. It lifts up a third of its body. It makes its neck get wider. It hisses loudly.

Many cobras eat small animals such as frogs, fishes, and birds. The cobra puts poison in its food as it chews.

Cobras-s-s!

Ricky
Name

Booklet Patterns

Lid

Cobras-s-s!

Basket

Name

©2000 The Education Center, Inc. • *I Can Make It! I Can Read It!* • Summer • TEC3508

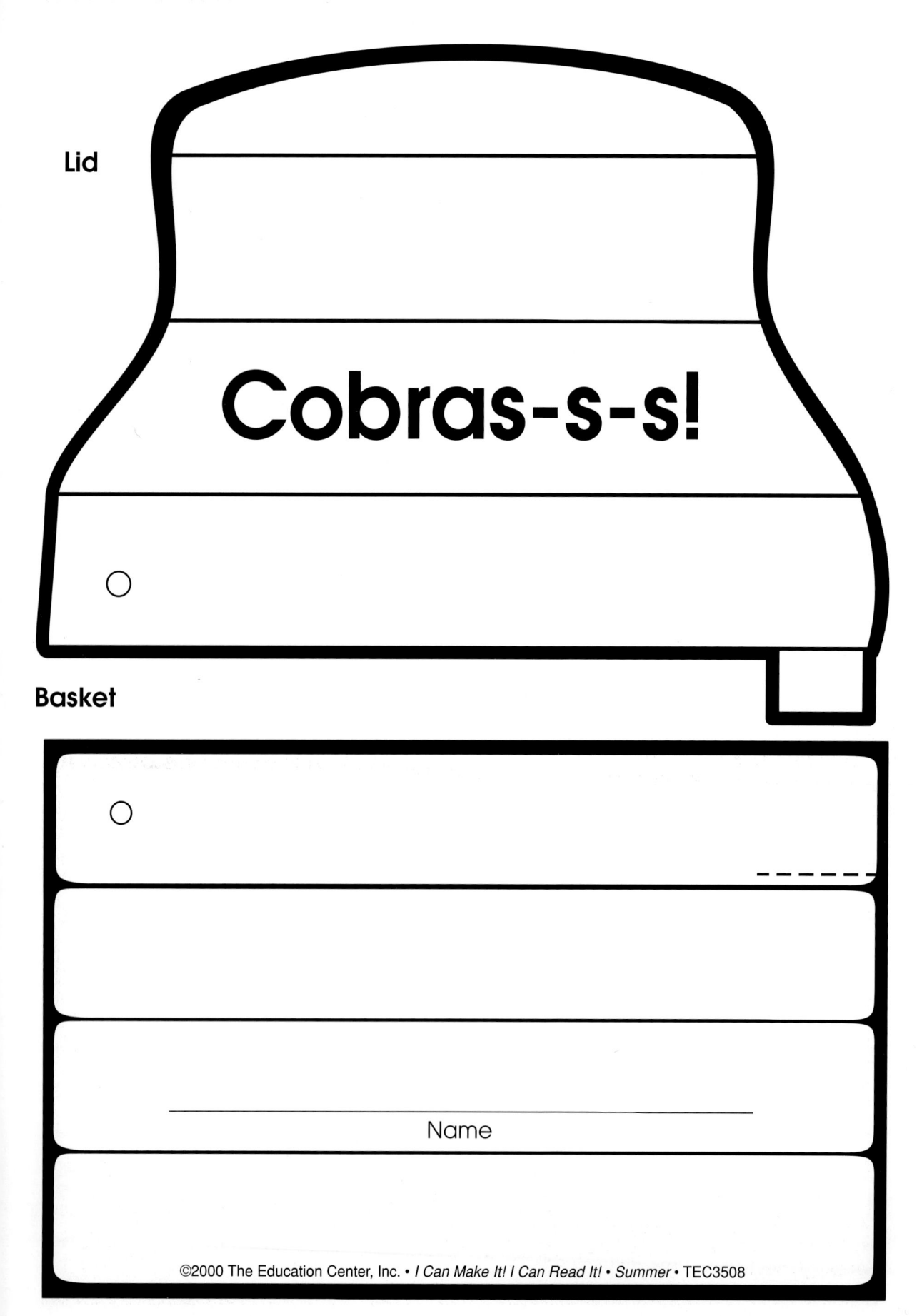

Note to the teacher: Use with "Cobras-s-s!" on page 51.

Booklet Patterns

Cobra Head

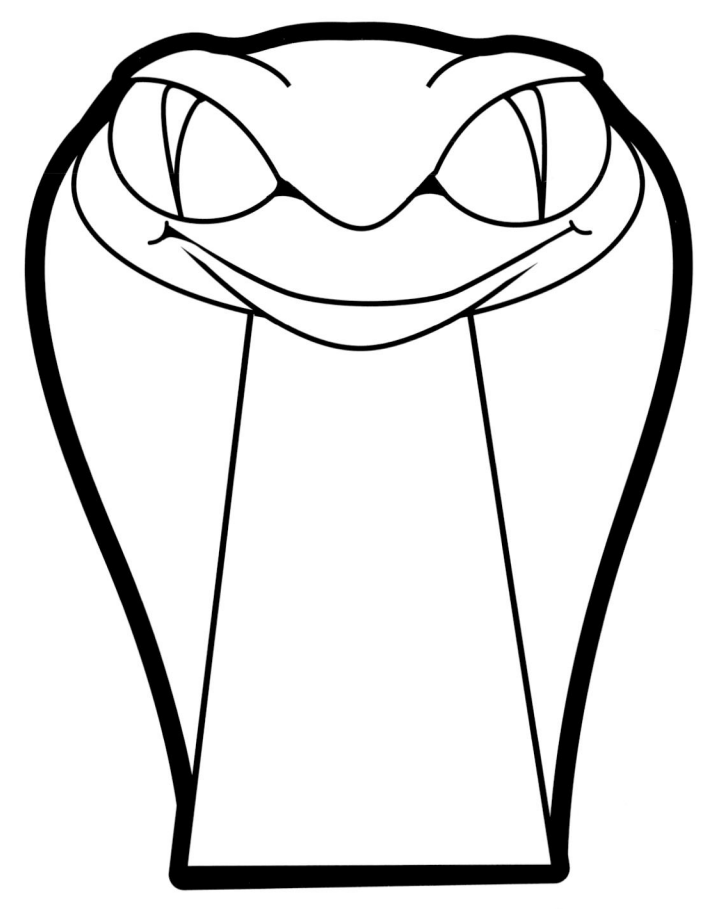

Basket Backing

Glue.

©2000 The Education Center, Inc. • *I Can Make It! I Can Read It!* • Summer • TEC3508

Note to the teacher: Use with "Cobras-s-s!" on page 51.

Booklet Patterns

Cobra Body

Glue.

A cobra is a poisonous snake that looks like it has a hood. Some cobras bite with their poisonous fangs. Other cobras squirt poison at the eyes of their enemies.

Cobras can be found in Africa and in parts of Asia. There are 12 kinds of cobras. The king cobra is the largest kind of cobra. It can grow to be 18 feet long.

A cobra does three things to get ready to fight. It lifts up a third of its body. It makes its neck get wider. It hisses loudly.

Many cobras eat small animals such as frogs, fishes, and birds. The cobra puts poison in its food as it chews.

Glue.

DOWN ON THE FARM

Cock-a-doodle-doo! Reading confidence will rise and shine with this circular farm booklet! Give each student a copy of pages 56–58 and a brad. Read with students the text on the bottom wheel, starting with the titled paragraph. Then have each student color her top wheel and animal pictures. Instruct her to cut out the booklet patterns along the bold outer lines. Next, direct her to glue each animal picture behind its matching text as illustrated. Have her use her brad to poke a hole through the top and bottom wheels where indicated. Instruct her to align the wheels as shown and insert the brad. Direct her to align the top wheel to reveal the titled paragraph and then practice reading the booklet with a buddy. Invite students to take their booklets home to read to family members and friends.

CREATIVE DECORATING OPTION

- Glue raffia, straw, or yarn below the farmer's feet.

To extend this booklet-making activity, read to students Denise Fleming's *Barnyard Banter* (Owlet, 1997).

Down on the Farm

Oink! Oink! Mother pig and her piglet squeal at the farmer. Are they calling for some corn to eat?

Betsy
Name

Booklet Pattern

Bottom Wheel

Down on the Farm
Oink! Oink! Mother pig and her piglet squeal at the farmer. Are they calling for some corn to eat?

Clop! Clop! Mother horse and her foal gallop up to the farmer. Are they hoping for hay to eat?

Moo! Moo! Mother cow and her calf moo at the farmer. Are they asking for grain to eat?

Sniff! Sniff! Mother goat and her kid sniff the farmer. Are they thinking about having the farmer's hat to eat?

Booklet Pattern

Top Wheel

Name

©2000 The Education Center, Inc.

©2000 The Education Center, Inc. • *I Can Make It! I Can Read It!* • *Summer* • TEC3508

Note to the teacher: Use with "Down on the Farm" on page 55.

Booklet Pattern

Animal Pictures

Glue.

Glue.

Glue.

Glue.

©2000 The Education Center, Inc. • *I Can Make It! I Can Read It!* • Summer • TEC3508

Note to the teacher: Use with "Down on the Farm" on page 55.

GOING ON SAFARI!

Send your youngsters on safari in search of reading fun with this accordion booklet! Give each student a copy of pages 60–62. Have the student color his patterns and then cut out the booklet patterns and pages on the bold outer lines. Instruct him to accordion-fold the booklet pages on the thin lines. Direct him to apply glue to Strip A and then press it to the back of the front cover. Next, have him apply glue to Strip B and press it to the back of the back cover so that when the pages are folded, the front and back elephants are aligned. Allow the glue to dry. Then read a completed booklet with students. Provide time for each student to read his booklet with a partner before he takes it home to read with family members.

CREATIVE DECORATING OPTION

- Glue wiggle eyes on the elephant.

To extend this booklet activity, invite a zookeeper to visit the class to talk about the care and habits of some of the animals.

Going on Safari!

I like to go on safari with my best friend, Zack.

We see lions napping in the cool shade,

We see monkeys swinging on the branches of tall trees.

Zack and I agree! There's nothing more fun to do.

We get to see the animals from an elephant's back.

And alligators watching the eggs they've laid.

And giraffes holding their heads high to catch a breeze.

We like to go on safari—at the city zoo!

Zack
Name

Booklet Pattern

Front Cover

Name

©2000 The Education Center, Inc. • *I Can Make It! I Can Read It!* • *Summer* • TEC3508

Note to the teacher: Use with "Going on Safari!" on page 59.

Back Cover

Booklet Pattern

©2000 The Education Center, Inc. • *I Can Make It! I Can Read It!* • Summer • TEC3508

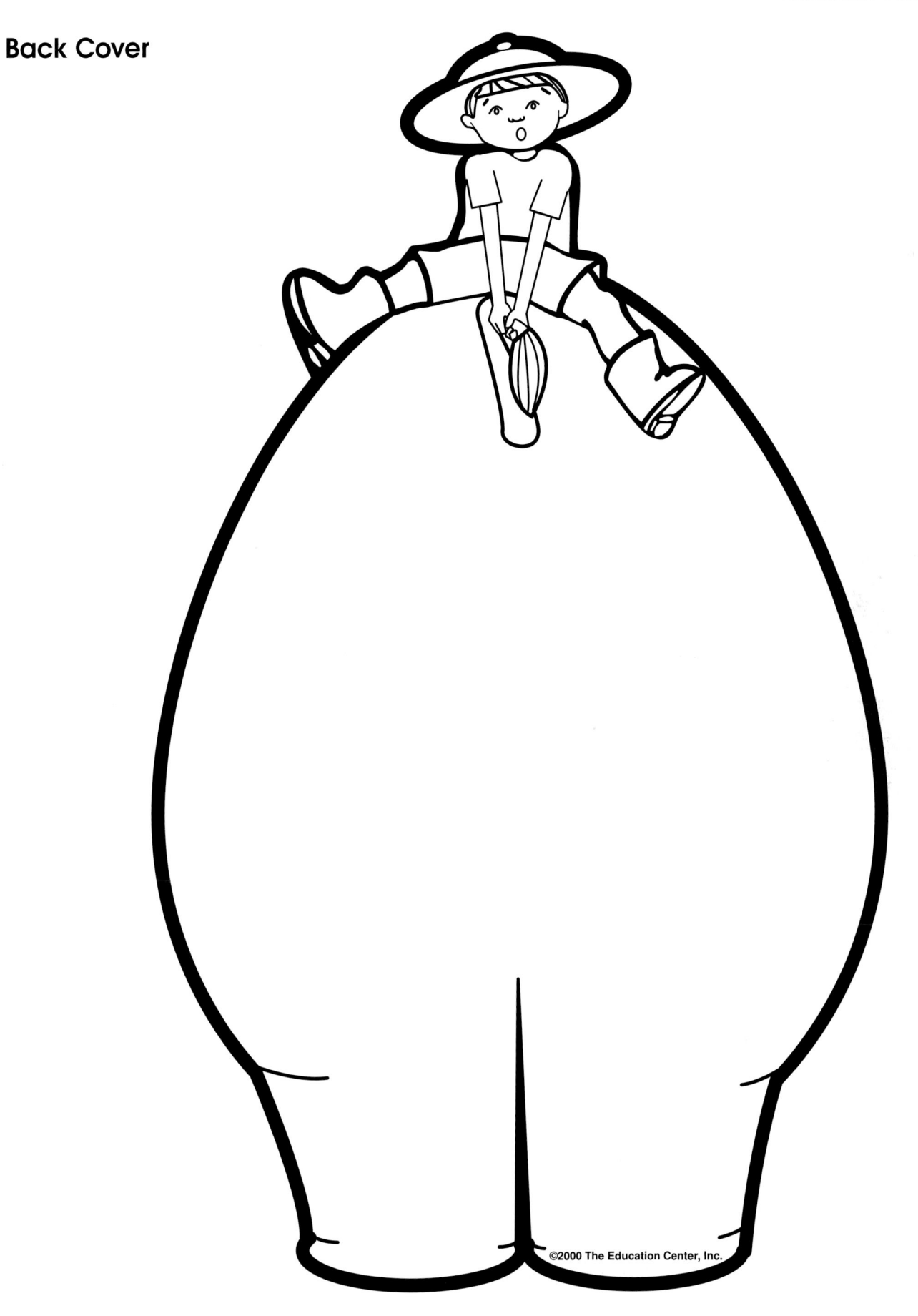

Note to the teacher: Use with "Going on Safari!" on page 59.

61

Booklet Pages

Strip B

Glue.

Zack and I agree! There's nothing more fun to do.

We like to go on safari—at the city zoo!

We see monkeys swinging on the branches of tall trees,

And giraffes holding their heads high to catch a breeze.

We see lions napping in the cool shade,

And alligators watching the eggs they've laid.

Going on Safari!

I like to go on safari with my best friend, Zack.

We get to see the animals from an elephant's back.

Strip A

Glue.

©2000 The Education Center, Inc. • *I Can Make It! I Can Read It!* • Summer • TEC3508

Note to the teacher: Use with "Going on Safari!" on page 59.

DEEP, DEEP, DEEPER

Your readers will discover new depths with this accordion ocean animal booklet! Give each student a copy of pages 64–66. Have the student color his booklet pages and then cut them out along the bold outer lines. Next, instruct him to glue the booklet pages together in numerical order. Demonstrate how to accordion-fold the pages along the thin black lines. (Start by folding the second block back.) Then read a completed booklet with students. Be sure to set aside time for each youngster to practice reading his booklet with a buddy. What a fun way to unfold the mysteries of the deep!

CREATIVE DECORATING OPTIONS

- Outline the ocean creatures with puffy paint.
- Glue sand to the ocean's edge.

To extend this booklet-making activity, read to students *Amazing Sea Creatures* by Andrew Brown (Crabtree Publishing, 1997).

Deep, Deep, Deeper

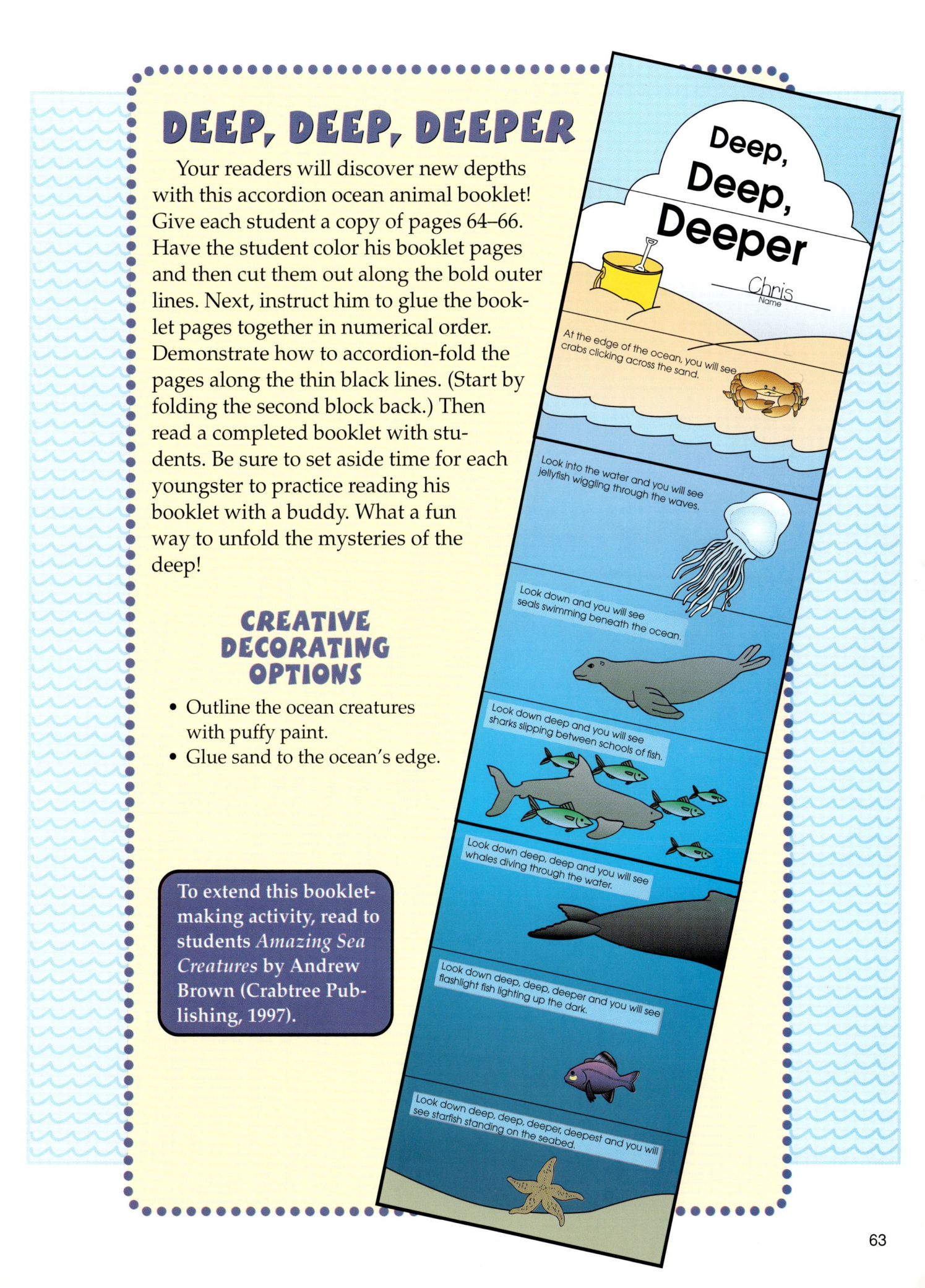

Name: Chris

At the edge of the ocean, you will see crabs clicking across the sand.

Look into the water and you will see jellyfish wiggling through the waves.

Look down and you will see seals swimming beneath the ocean.

Look down deep and you will see sharks slipping between schools of fish.

Look down deep, deep and you will see whales diving through the water.

Look down deep, deep, deeper and you will see flashlight fish lighting up the dark.

Look down deep, deep, deeper, deepest and you will see starfish standing on the seabed.

63

Booklet Pages

Deep, Deep, Deeper

_____
Name

At the edge of the ocean, you will see crabs clicking across the sand.

1

©2000 The Education Center, Inc. • *I Can Make It! I Can Read It!* • Summer • TEC3508

64 **Note to the teacher:** Use with "Deep, Deep, Deeper" on page 63.

Booklet Pages

Glue.

Look into the water and you will see jellyfish wiggling through the waves.

2

Look down and you will see seals swimming beneath the ocean.

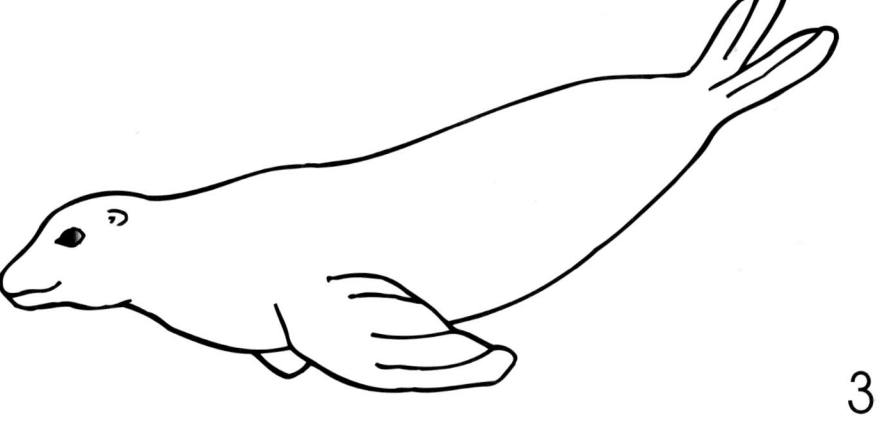

3

Look down deep and you will see sharks slipping between schools of fish.

4

©2000 The Education Center, Inc. • *I Can Make It! I Can Read It!* • Summer • TEC3508

Note to the teacher: Use with "Deep, Deep, Deeper" on page 63.

Booklet Pages

Glue.

Look down deep, deep and you will see whales diving through the water.

5

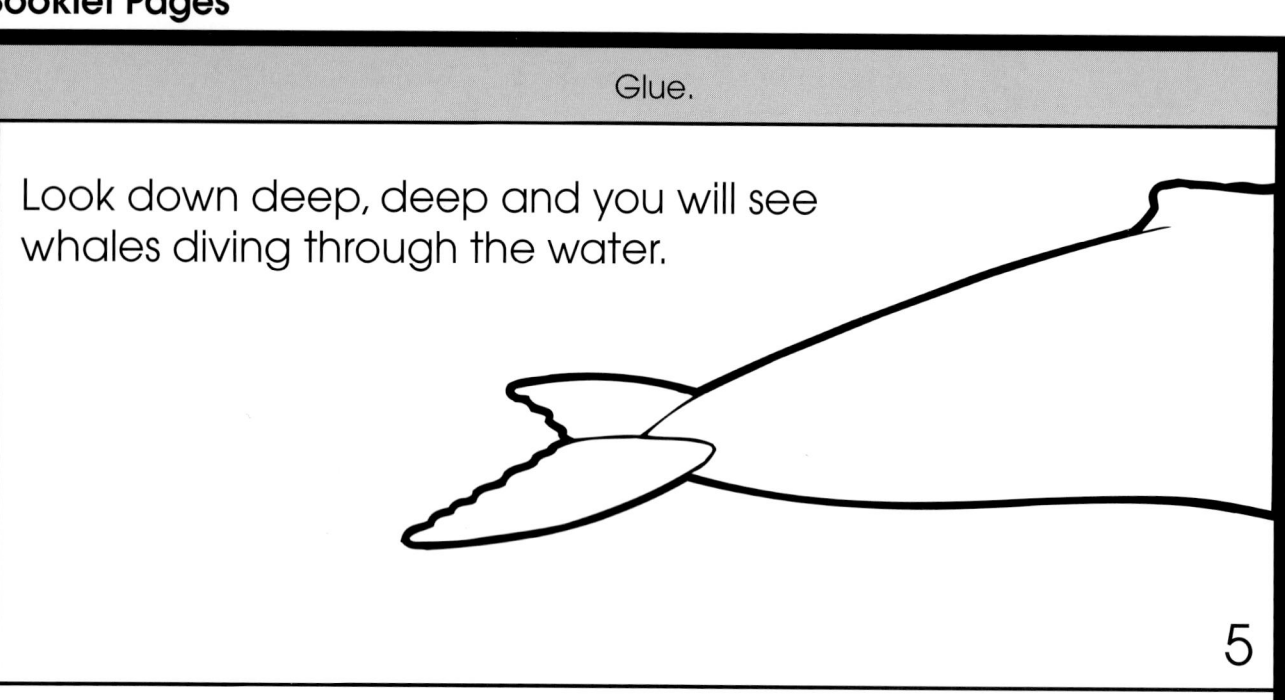

Look down deep, deep, deeper and you will see flashlight fish lighting up the dark.

6

Look down deep, deep, deeper, deepest and you will see starfish standing on the seabed.

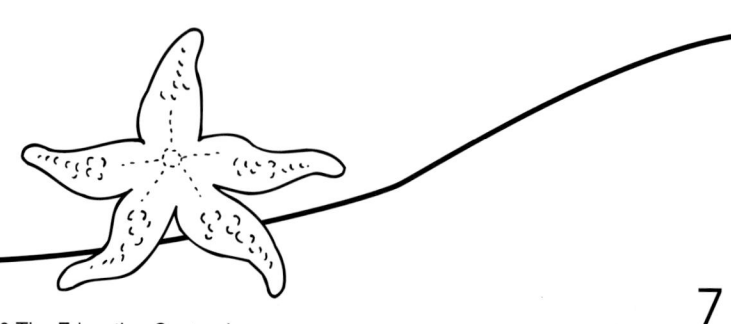

7

©2000 The Education Center, Inc.

HOWDY, PARTNER!

Yee-haw! It's hats off to the Old West with this informative booklet! Give each student a tagboard copy of pages 68–69, a white copy of pages 70–72, and a brad. Have the student color and cut out her booklet backing, cover, pages, and pattern. Direct her to stack her booklet pages in numerical order, placing the cover on top. Align the pages with the top of the head on the backing and staple at the upper left. Next, punch holes in the backing and hat pattern where indicated. Have the student insert the brad through both holes as illustrated. Demonstrate how to rotate the arm so that the hat covers the top of the head and is secured behind the left ear. Next, read a completed booklet with students. Provide time for each student to read her booklet with a partner before she takes it home to read with family members. Steering youngsters into reading has never been so easy!

CREATIVE DECORATING OPTIONS

- Glue a sheriff's badge made of construction paper to the cowboy's left shoulder. Label the badge "Sheriff [student's name]."
- Outline the hat with glue. Sprinkle the glue with sand.

To extend this booklet activity, have an adventure at a dude ranch by reading aloud *On the Trail With Miss Pace* by Sharon Phillips Denslow (Simon & Schuster Books for Young Readers, 1995).

Booklet Backing

©2000 The Education Center, Inc. • *I Can Make It! I Can Read It!* • Summer • TEC3508

68 **Note to the teacher:** Use with "Howdy, Partner!" on page 67.

Booklet Pattern

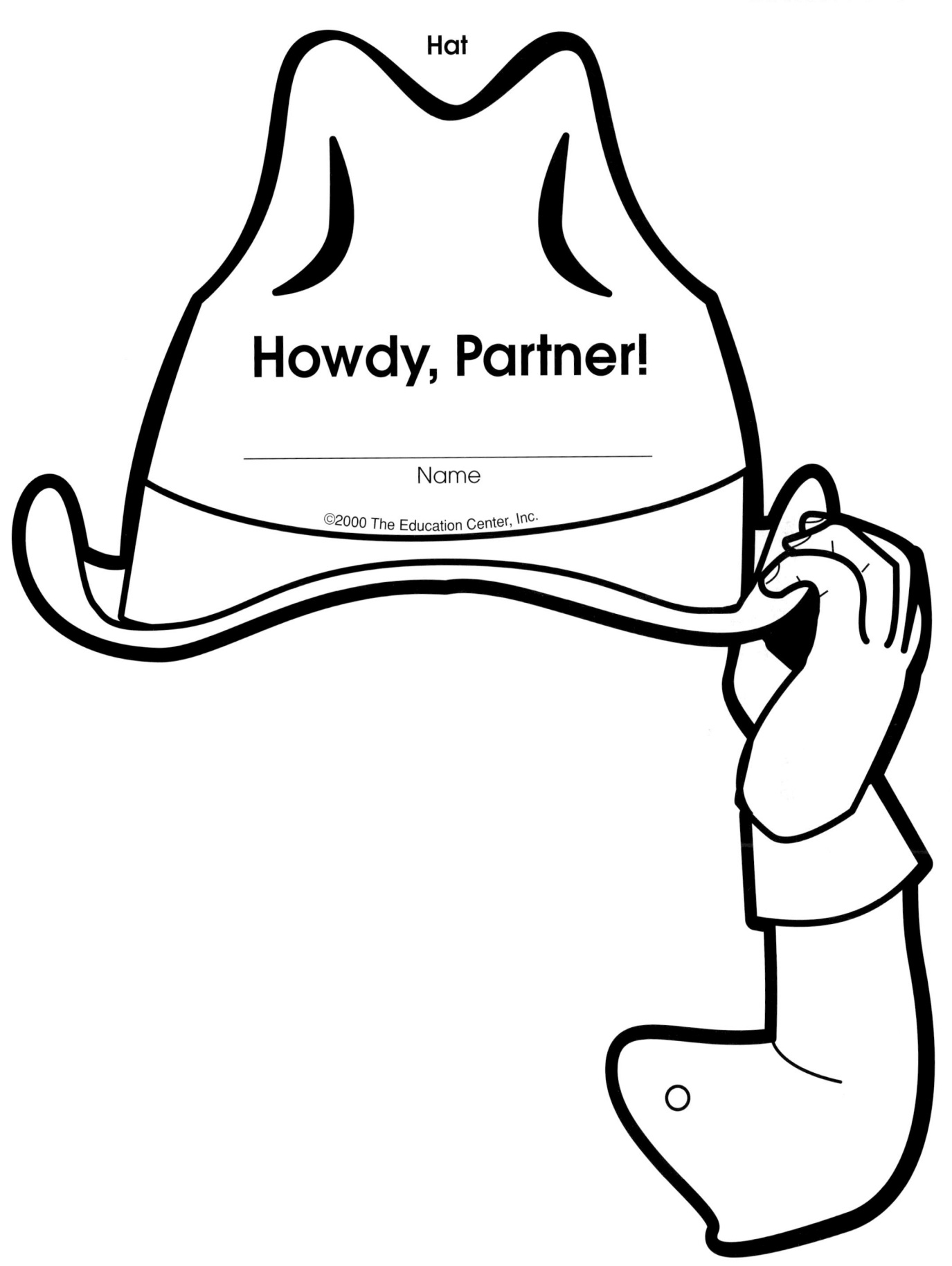

Hat

Howdy, Partner!

Name

©2000 The Education Center, Inc.

©2000 The Education Center, Inc. • *I Can Make It! I Can Read It!* • Summer • TEC3508

Note to the teacher: Use with "Howdy, Partner!" on page 67.

Booklet Cover and Pages

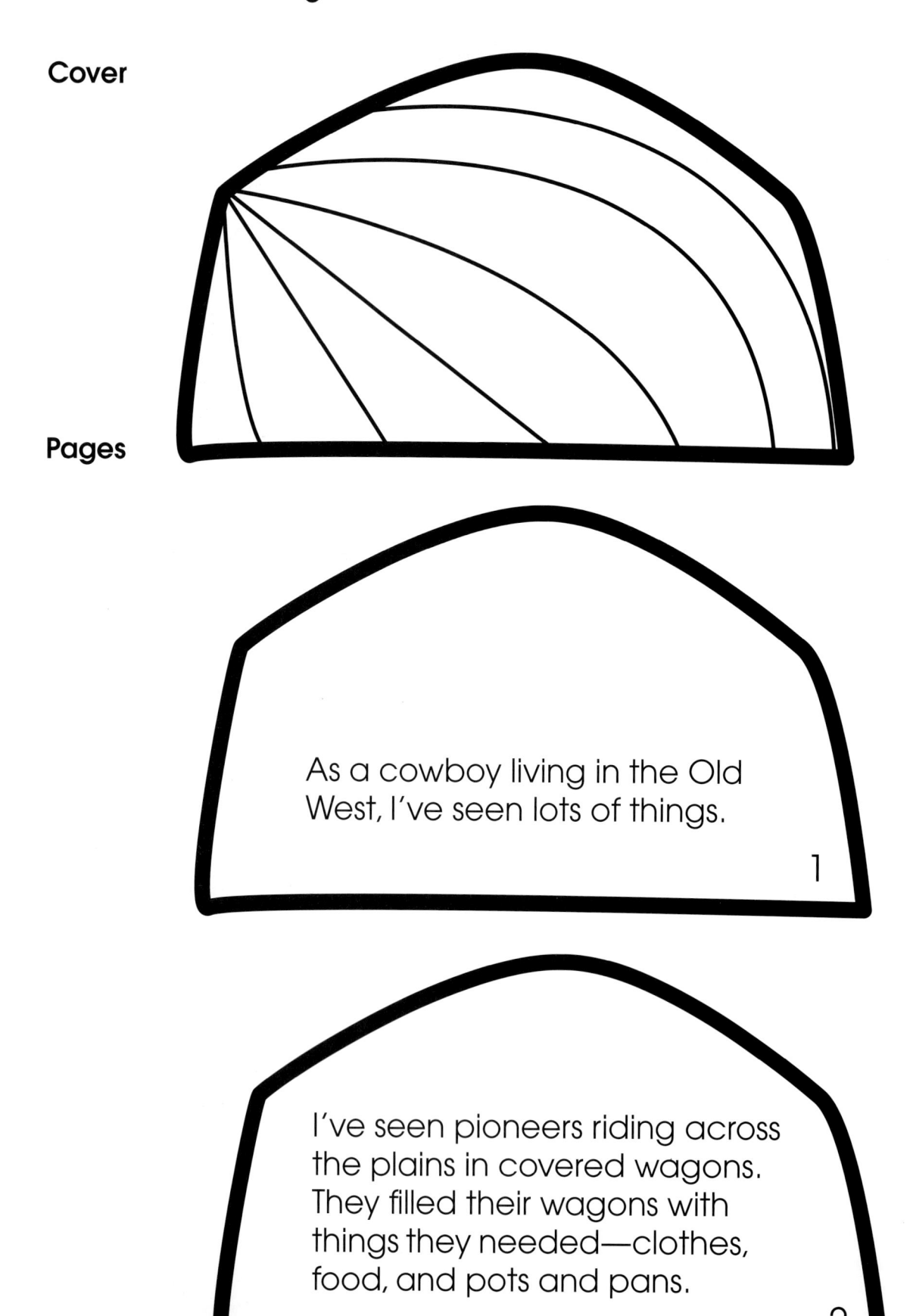

Cover

Pages

As a cowboy living in the Old West, I've seen lots of things.

1

I've seen pioneers riding across the plains in covered wagons. They filled their wagons with things they needed—clothes, food, and pots and pans.

2

Booklet Pages

I've seen Pony Express riders racing across the plains on horses. They rode 75 miles a day, just to bring a letter!

3

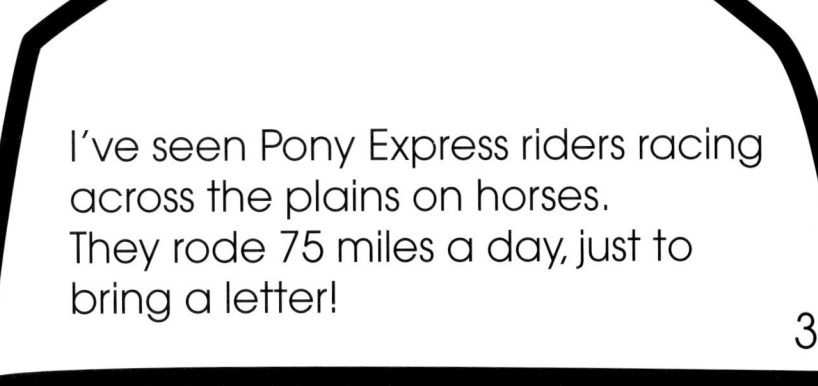

I've seen cowboys driving cattle to market and working on ranches. They twirled their ropes and lassoed the cattle as quick as one, two, three!

4

I've seen gunslingers and sharpshooters, good guys and bad guys. The best of them could shoot a playing card in half at 30 paces!

5

©2000 The Education Center, Inc. • *I Can Make It! I Can Read It!* • *Summer* • TEC3508

Note to the teacher: Use with "Howdy, Partner!" on page 67.

Booklet Pages

I've seen tribes of Plains Indians camped beside rivers. They set up their teepees in a circle and played drums that sounded like heartbeats.

6

I've seen great herds of buffalo thundering across the plains. When thousands of them swam across a river, boats had to stop to let them pass.

7

What about you, partner? What kinds of things do you see where you live?

8

CITY VIEWS APARTMENTS

What do you see from the windows of city apartments? Discover the answers with this homey flip booklet! Give each student a copy of pages 74–76. To make the booklet, the student cuts out the booklet pages and colors the illustrations of the children. Then he cuts out the dotted boxes to create windows. Next, he glues his booklet pages together where indicated to make one long strip. He cuts along the dotted lines to create flaps. He folds the resulting flaps so the windows reveal the illustrations and then he secures the tabs. Next, he colors and cuts out his booklet patterns. He glues the roof to the outside of his booklet and the door to the bottom right-hand corner. He glues the tree trunk to the left side of the door, making sure the top of the tree is free of glue. Lastly, he glues the sign to the flap above the tree. To read a completed booklet, the student starts with the text behind the bottom flap and finishes with the top flap. Provide time for each student to practice reading his booklet with a partner before inviting him to take it home to read to family members.

CREATIVE DECORATING OPTIONS

- Glue shutters made from scraps of construction paper to the booklet front.
- Draw and color a picture of the apartment building landlord on the inside of the bottom flap.

To extend this booklet activity, meet Walter's neighbors as he and his bed plummet through his apartment building. Read aloud *No Jumping on the Bed* by Tedd Arnold (Dial Books for Young Readers, 1987).

Booklet Pages

Hello! I'm Jill. From my window I see the tops of the trees on the city street.

Hi! I'm Ricky. From my window I see the busy traffic of the city.

Welcome to City Views Apartments! The people in these apartments like their special views of the city. Come on up and meet them. They'll tell you what they see!

©2000 The Education Center, Inc. • I Can Make It! I Can Read It! • Summer • TEC3508

©2000 The Education Center, Inc. • I Can Make It! I Can Read It! • Summer • TEC3508

74   **Note to the teacher:** Use with "City Views Apartments" on page 73.

Booklet Pages

Hello! I'm Sam. From my window I see the stars and moon above the city.

Hi! I'm Tom. From my window I see the bright lights of the city.

Hello! I'm Sue. From my window I see the tall buildings of the city.

Glue here.

©2000 The Education Center, Inc. • *I Can Make It! I Can Read It!* • Summer • TEC3508

Note to the teacher: Use with "City Views Apartments" on page 73.

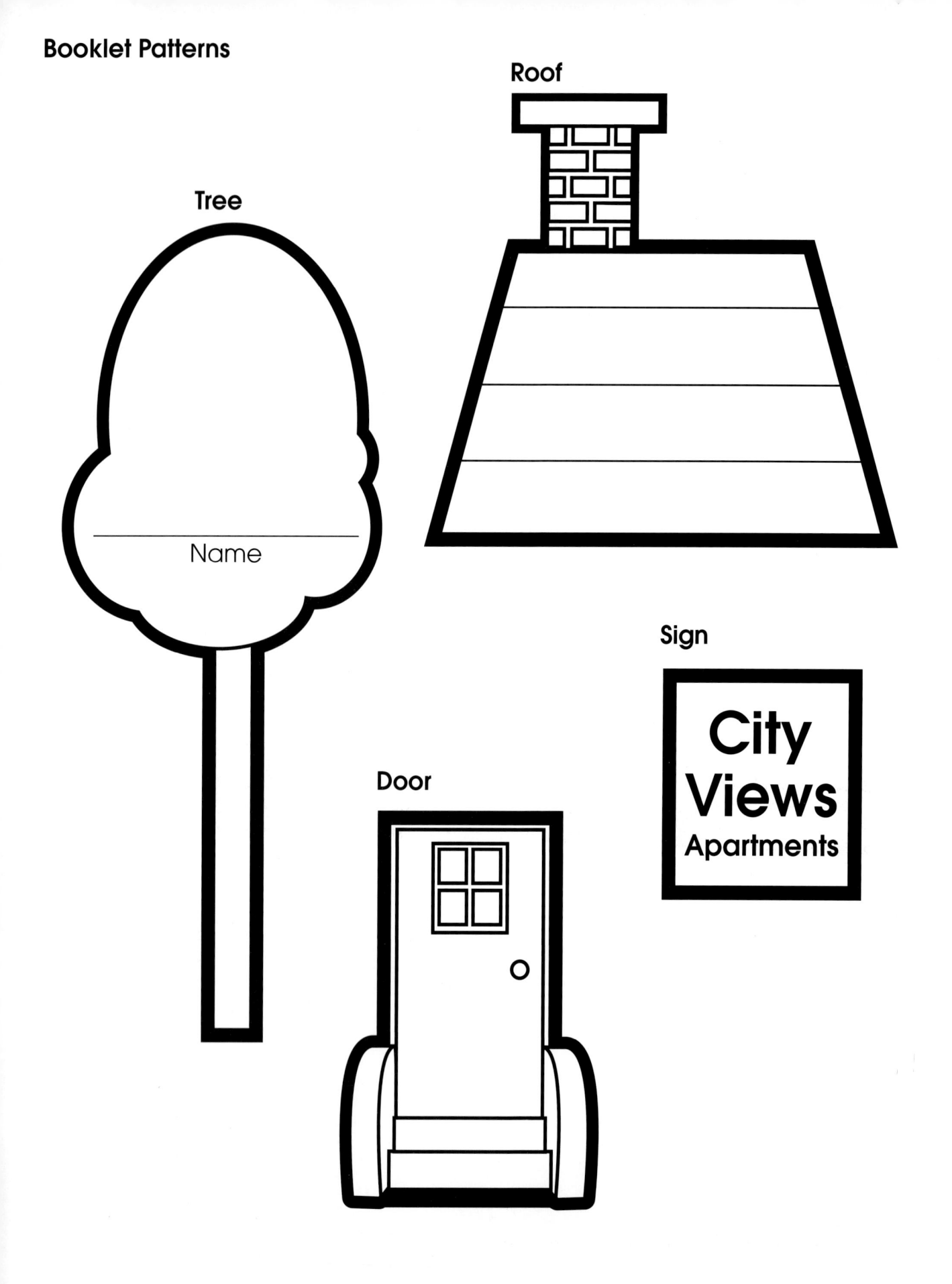

Booklet Patterns

Tree

Roof

Name

Door

Sign

City Views Apartments

©2000 The Education Center, Inc. • *I Can Make It! I Can Read It!* • Summer • TEC3508

Note to the teacher: Use with "City Views Apartments" on page 73.

A WALK IN THE COUNTRY

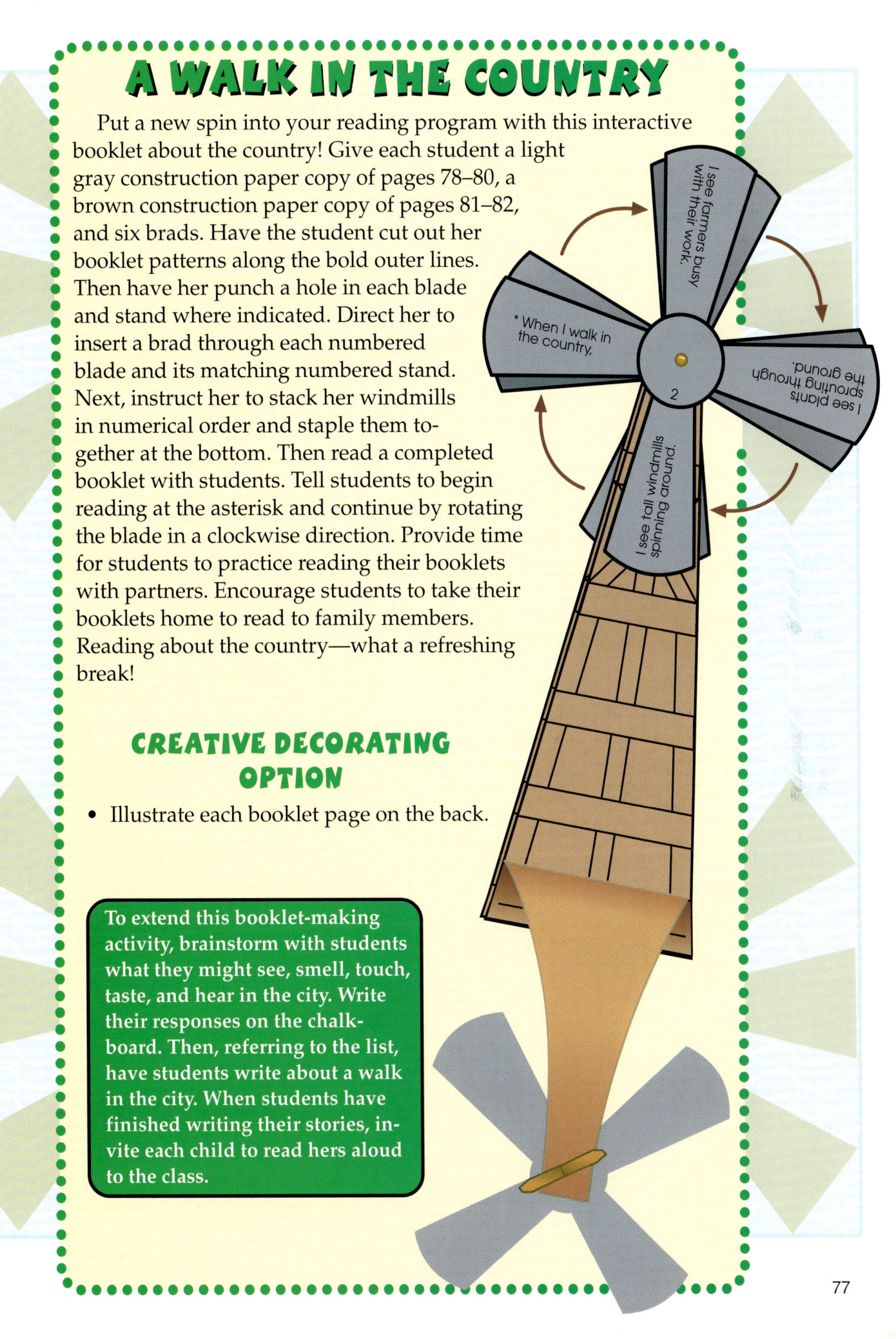

Put a new spin into your reading program with this interactive booklet about the country! Give each student a light gray construction paper copy of pages 78–80, a brown construction paper copy of pages 81–82, and six brads. Have the student cut out her booklet patterns along the bold outer lines. Then have her punch a hole in each blade and stand where indicated. Direct her to insert a brad through each numbered blade and its matching numbered stand. Next, instruct her to stack her windmills in numerical order and staple them together at the bottom. Then read a completed booklet with students. Tell students to begin reading at the asterisk and continue by rotating the blade in a clockwise direction. Provide time for students to practice reading their booklets with partners. Encourage students to take their booklets home to read to family members. Reading about the country—what a refreshing break!

CREATIVE DECORATING OPTION

- Illustrate each booklet page on the back.

To extend this booklet-making activity, brainstorm with students what they might see, smell, touch, taste, and hear in the city. Write their responses on the chalkboard. Then, referring to the list, have students write about a walk in the city. When students have finished writing their stories, invite each child to read hers aloud to the class.

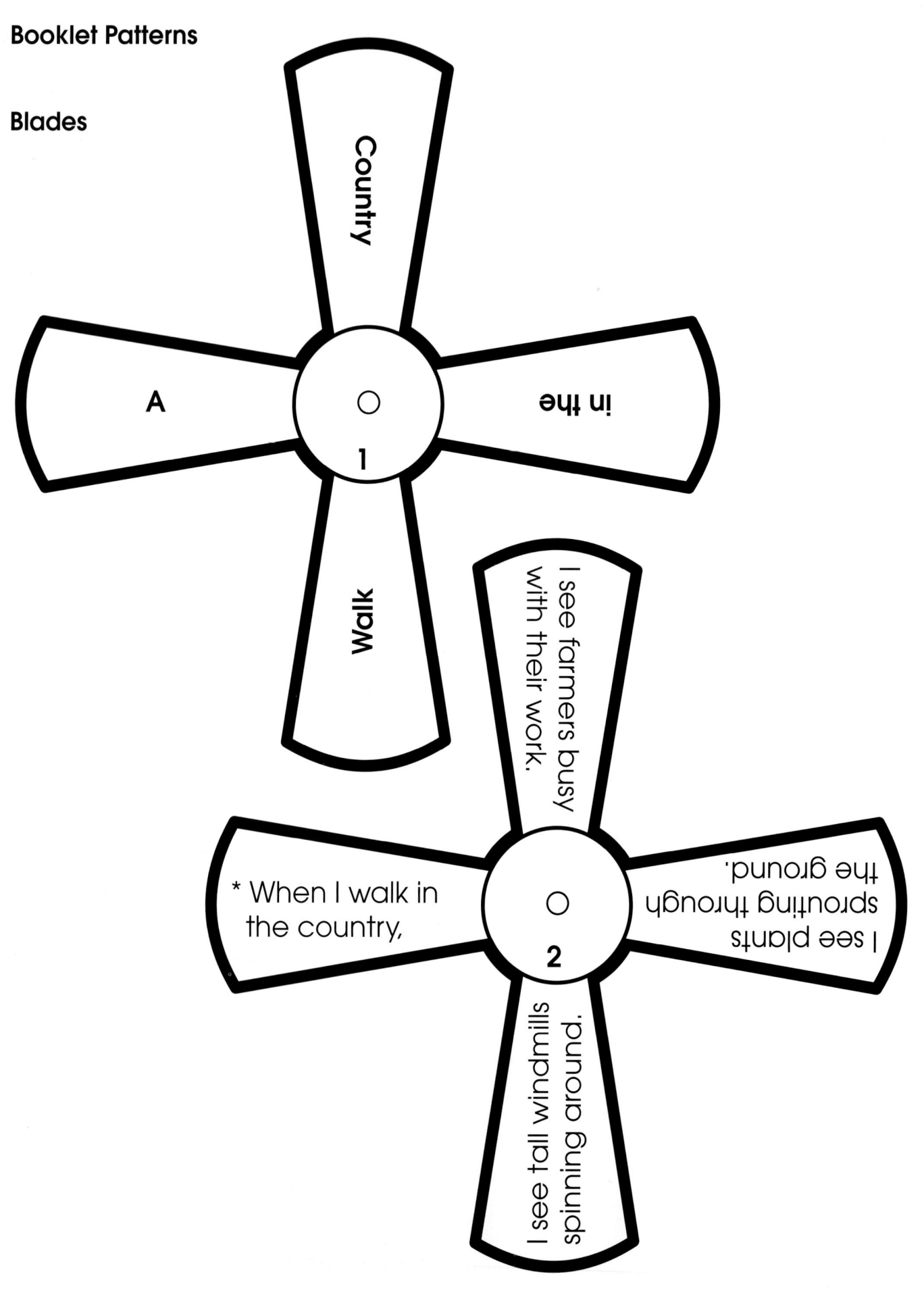

Booklet Patterns

Blades

Country

A

in the

1

Walk

I see farmers busy with their work.

* When I walk in the country,

I see plants sprouting through the ground.

2

I see tall windmills spinning around.

©2000 The Education Center, Inc. • *I Can Make It! I Can Read It!* • Summer • TEC3508

Note to the teacher: Use with "A Walk in the Country" on page 77.

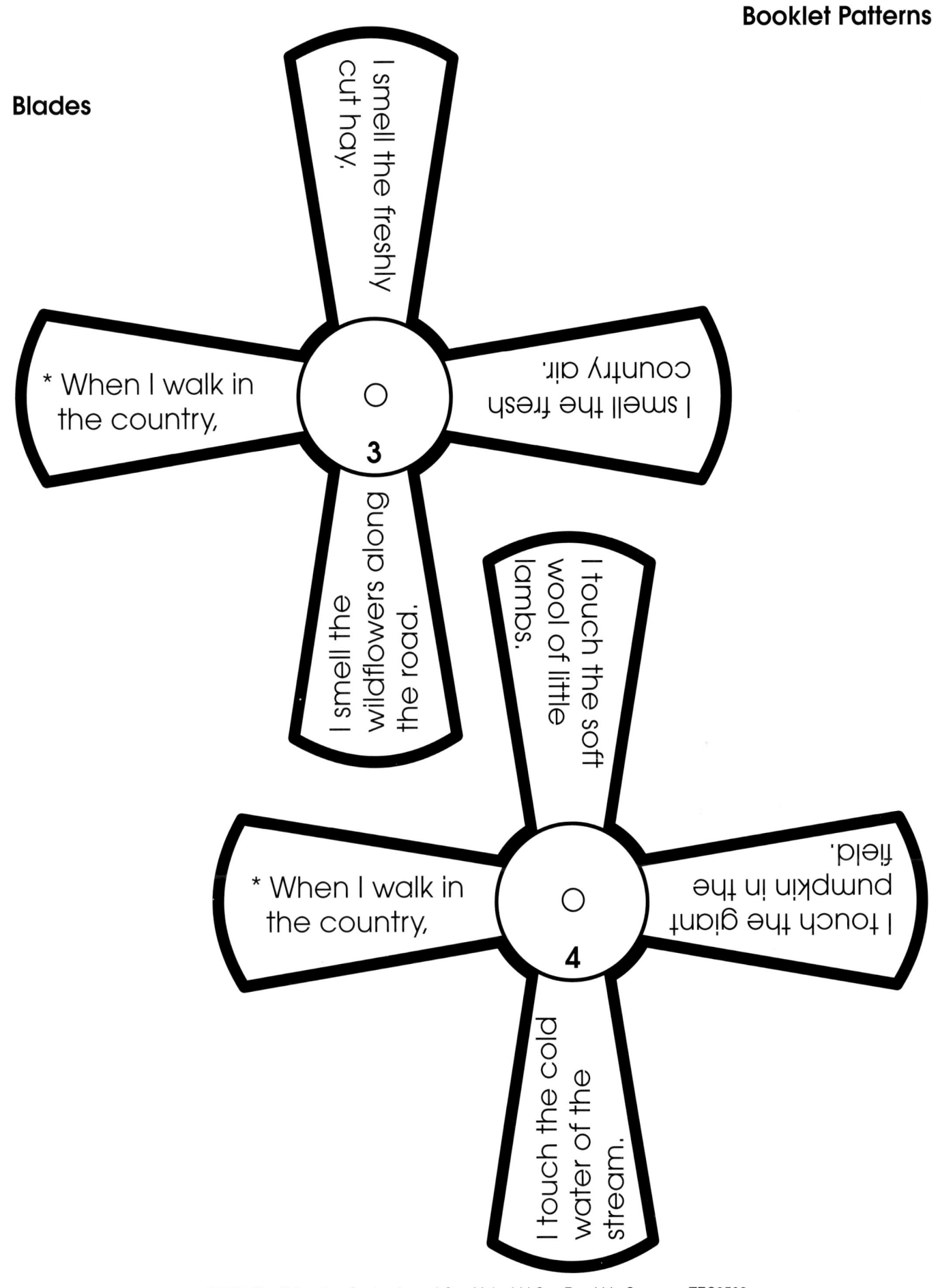

Booklet Patterns

Blades

Pinwheel 3:
- * When I walk in the country,
- I smell the freshly cut hay.
- I smell the fresh country air.
- I smell the wildflowers along the road.

Pinwheel 4:
- * When I walk in the country,
- I touch the soft wool of little lambs.
- I touch the giant pumpkin in the field.
- I touch the cold water of the stream.

©2000 The Education Center, Inc. • *I Can Make It! I Can Read It!* • Summer • TEC3508

Note to the teacher: Use with "A Walk in the Country" on page 77.

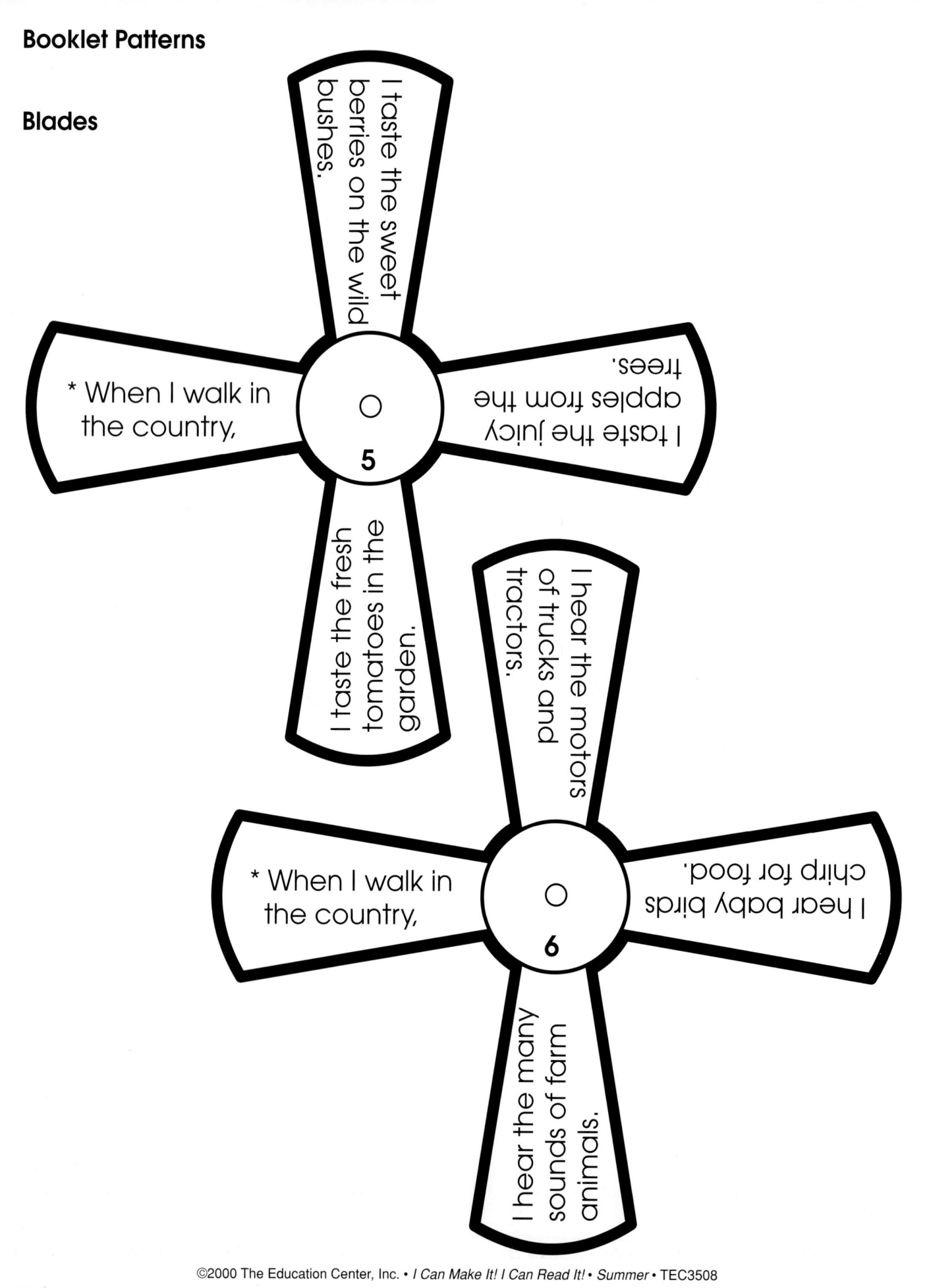

Booklet Patterns

Blades

Blade 5:
- * When I walk in the country,
- I taste the sweet berries on the wild bushes.
- I taste the juicy apples from the trees.
- I taste the fresh tomatoes in the garden.

Blade 6:
- * When I walk in the country,
- I hear the motors of trucks and tractors.
- I hear baby birds chirp for food.
- I hear the many sounds of farm animals.

©2000 The Education Center, Inc. • *I Can Make It! I Can Read It!* • Summer • TEC3508

Note to the teacher: Use with "A Walk in the Country" on page 77.

Stands

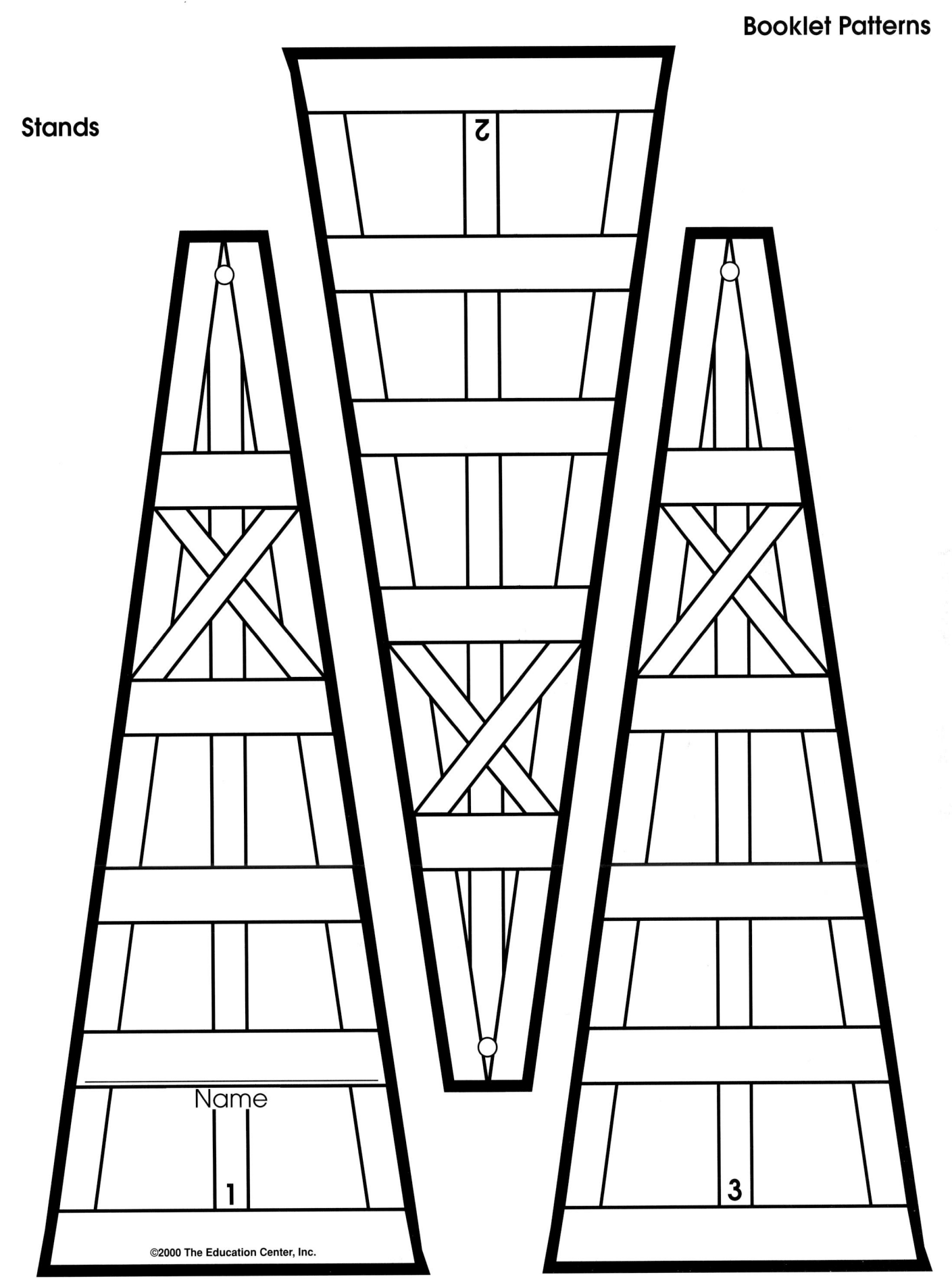

Booklet Patterns

Name

1

2

3

©2000 The Education Center, Inc.

©2000 The Education Center, Inc. • *I Can Make It! I Can Read It!* • Summer • TEC3508

Note to the teacher: Use with "A Walk in the Country" on page 77.

81

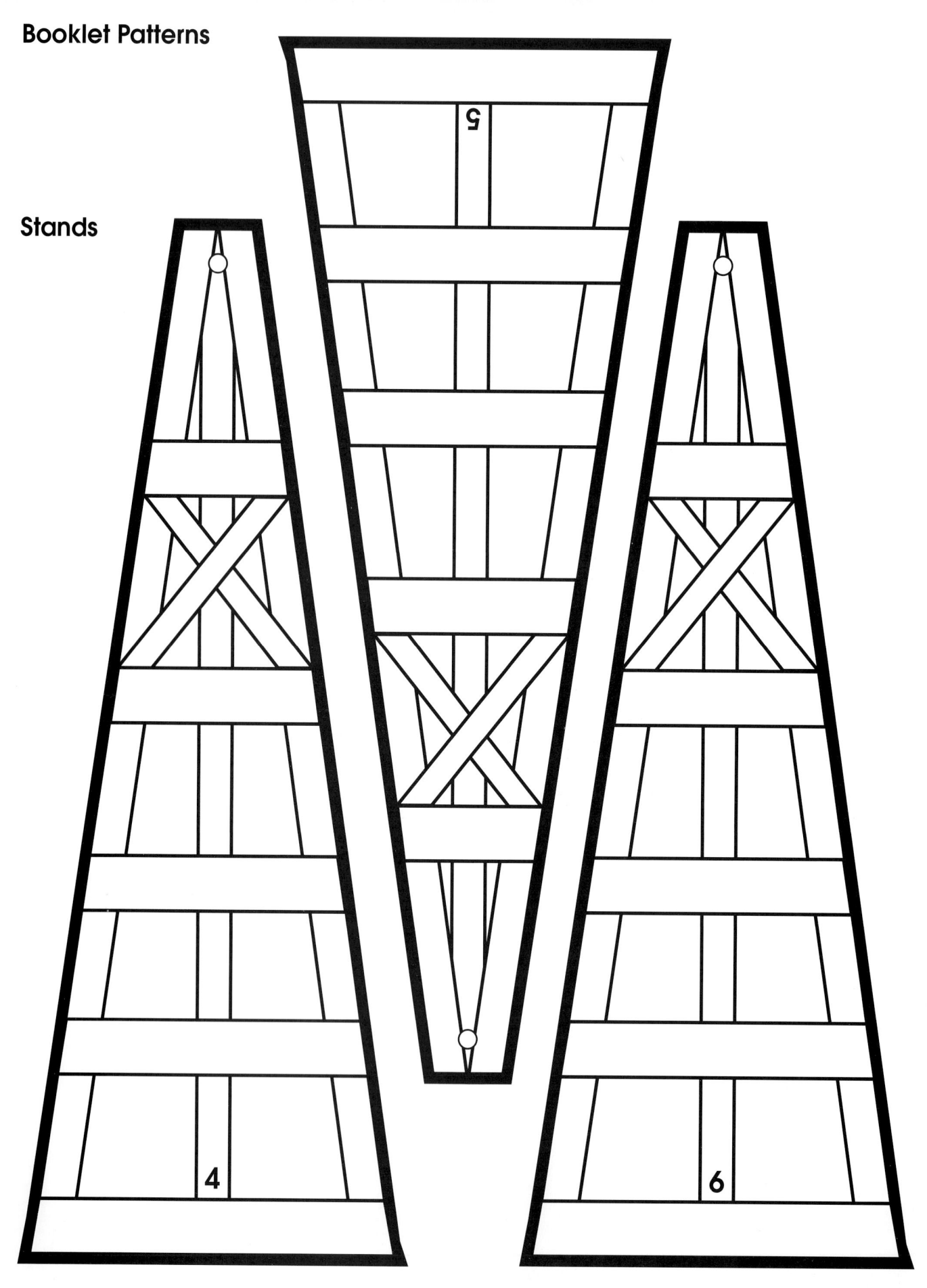

Booklet Patterns

Stands

©2000 The Education Center, Inc. • *I Can Make It! I Can Read It!* • *Summer* • TEC3508

82 **Note to the teacher:** Use with "A Walk in the Country" on page 77.

STORM WATCH!

Electrify your reading program with this rhyming thunder and lightning booklet! Give each student a copy of pages 85–86 and a gray construction paper copy of page 84. Have the student color his booklet patterns and sunny booklet page, reminding him to color lightly over the text so the booklet can be read. Next, instruct him to cut out his booklet patterns and pages. Then have him glue the rain pattern to the back of the storm page between the dotted lines and the lightning between the two solid lines as shown. Next, instruct him to align the two booklet pages back-to-back and staple them together at the top. When the glue has dried, have him fold the rain and lightning patterns back between the two booklet pages. Read a completed booklet with students, demonstrating how to unfold each pattern when its matching sentence is read. Refold the patterns before turning over the booklet to finish reading. Then provide time for each student to read his booklet with a partner. Encourage students to take their booklets home to read to family members. It may be stormy outside, but inside, the reading is smooth and sunny!

CREATIVE DECORATING OPTIONS

- Add glitter to the lightning bolt.
- Color birds flying in the clouds of the sunny booklet page.

Extend this booklet activity by reading aloud the Nigerian folktale *The Story of Lightning and Thunder* by Ashley Bryan (Aladdin Paperbacks, 1999).

Storm Watch!

First, the clouds turn dark and gray
And we know rain is on the way.

Then the rain begins to pour
And the thunder starts to roar!

Next, the sky is all aglow
As the lightning puts on a flashy show.

Finally the storm has passed
And sunny skies are here at last!

Stormy Booklet Page

Storm Watch!

First, the clouds turn dark and gray
And we know rain is on the way.

Then the rain begins to pour
And the thunder starts to roar!

Next, the sky is all aglow
As the lightning puts on a flashy show.

©2000 The Education Center, Inc. • *I Can Make It! I Can Read It!* • *Summer* • TEC3508

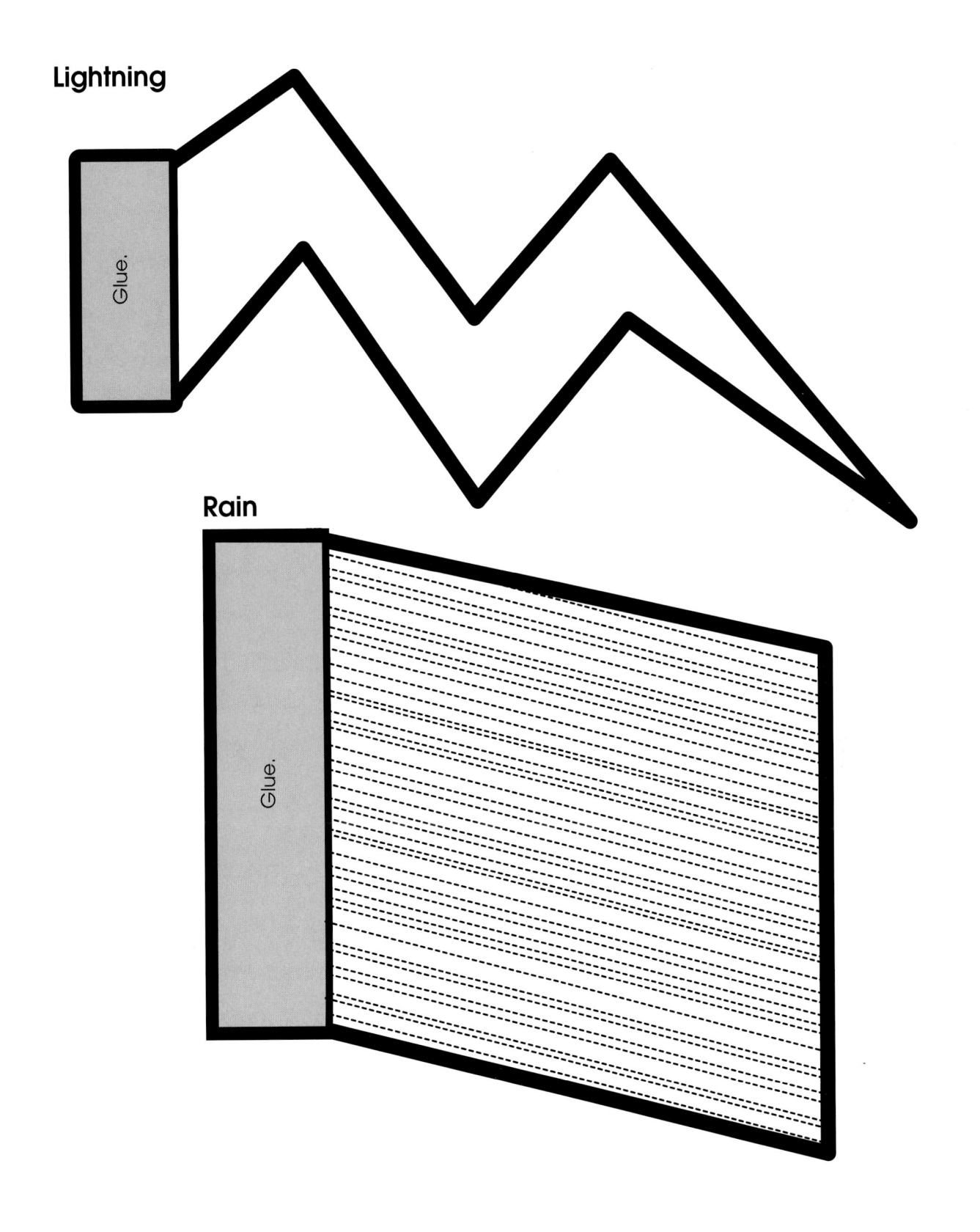

Booklet Patterns

Lightning

Glue.

Rain

Glue.

©2000 The Education Center, Inc. • *I Can Make It! I Can Read It!* • Summer • TEC3508

Note to the teacher: Use with "Storm Watch!" on page 83.

85

Sunny Booklet Page

Finally the storm has passed
And sunny skies are here at last!

Name _____

©2000 The Education Center, Inc. • *I Can Make It! I Can Read It!* • *Summer* • TEC3508

Note to the teacher: Use with "Storm Watch!" on page 83.

UP IN THE AIR OVER PLANES

Give your reading program a lift with this aviation booklet! Give each student a copy of pages 88–92 and a brad. Have the student color and cut out her cover, booklet pages, and pattern. For booklet pages 1–4, have her staple each plane to its matching cloud by placing the plane nose flush to the left edge of the cloud (see the illustration). For booklet page 5, have her position the plane nose next to the cloud's circle and then staple. Next, instruct her to stack her booklet pages in numerical order and staple them together at the top. Punch a hole through the cloud's circle and the center of the propeller. Help her insert the brad through the propeller and cloud, with the propeller overlapping the cover. Then read a completed booklet with students. Provide time for each student to practice reading with a partner. Encourage students to take their booklets home to read to family members and friends. Parents will love how their children's reading is taking off!

CREATIVE DECORATING OPTIONS

- Draw faces in the plane windows.
- Use blue liquid tempera paint and a sponge to dab a design on the clouds.

To extend this booklet activity, make a template of the plane pattern. Have each student trace the template and cut out the shape. Then have the student write about where she would like a plane to take her. Display the work on a bulletin board titled "From Here to There!"

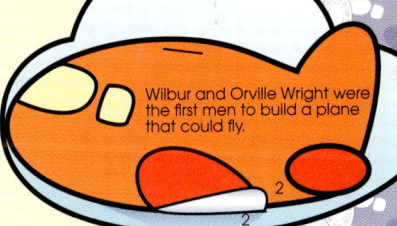

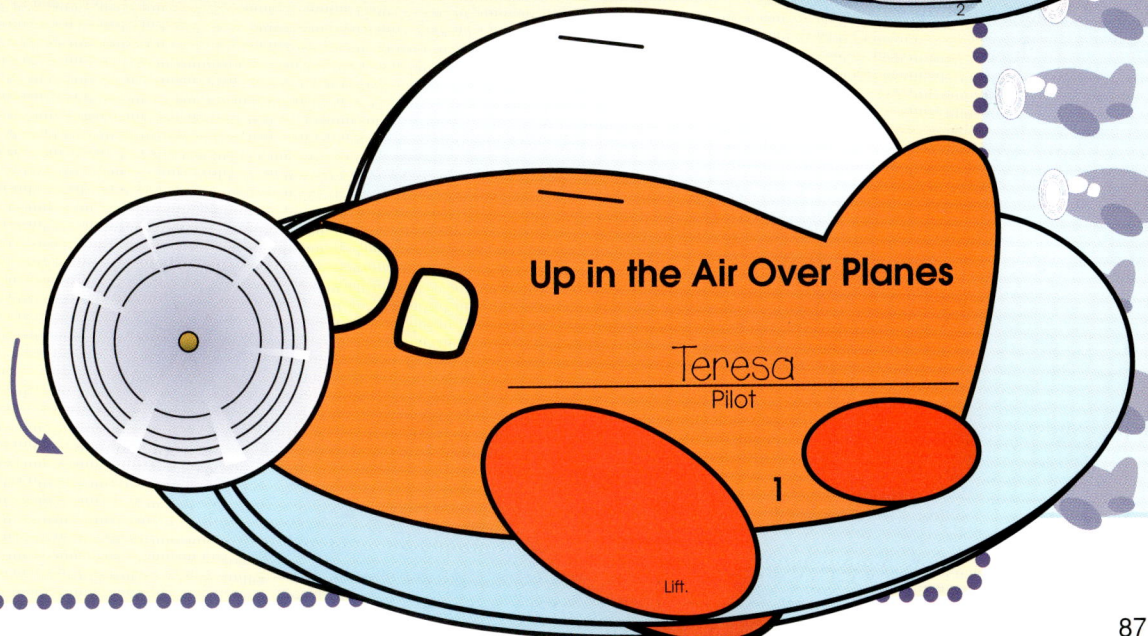

Wilbur and Orville Wright were the first men to build a plane that could fly.

Up in the Air Over Planes

Teresa
Pilot

Lift.

Booklet Page and Cover

Booklet Page

Who were the first men to build a plane that could fly?

1

Cover

Up in the Air Over Planes

Pilot

1

Lift.

Booklet Pages

Why do some farmers use planes?

2

Wilbur and Orville Wright were the first men to build a plane that could fly.

2

Lift.

Booklet Pages

How do planes help people who live far from cities and towns?

3

Farmers use planes to spray their crops, count their animals, and plant seeds in their fields.

3

Lift.

Booklet Pages

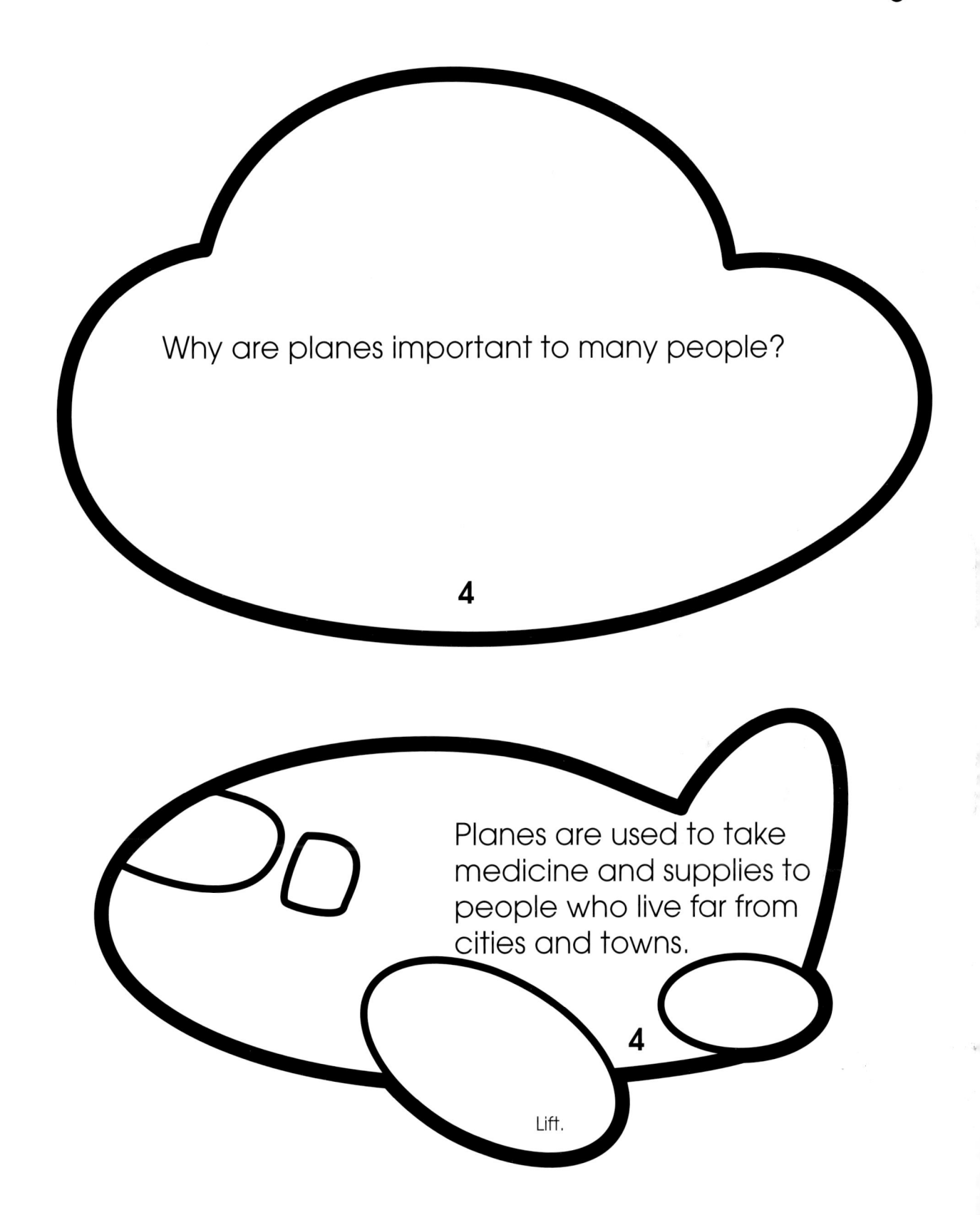

Why are planes important to many people?

4

Planes are used to take medicine and supplies to people who live far from cities and towns.

4

Lift.

©2000 The Education Center, Inc. • *I Can Make It! I Can Read It!* • Summer • TEC3508

Note to the teacher: Use with "Up in the Air Over Planes" on page 87.

Booklet Pages and Pattern

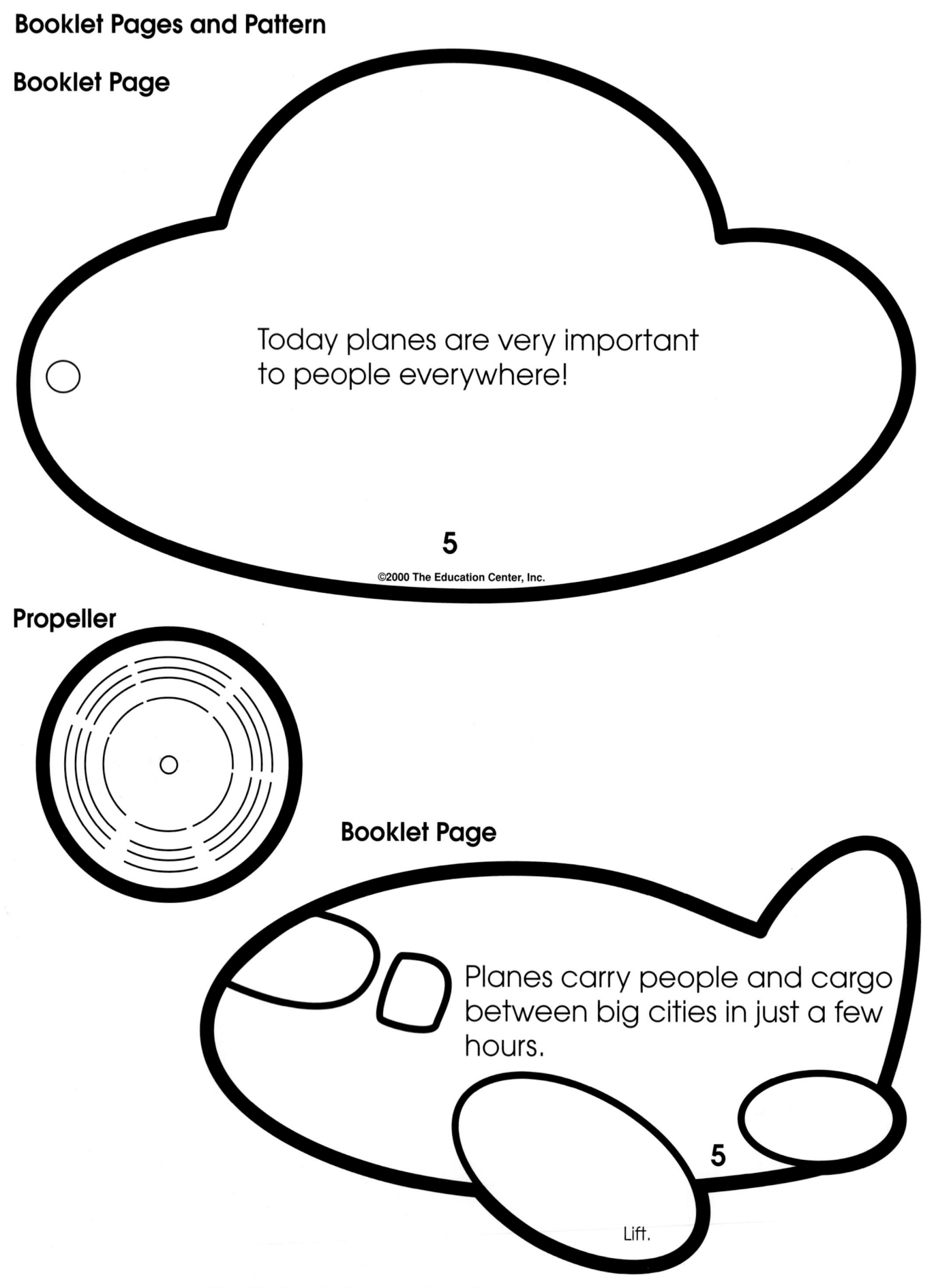

Booklet Page

Today planes are very important to people everywhere!

5

Propeller

Booklet Page

Planes carry people and cargo between big cities in just a few hours.

5

Lift.